Pot Black

Pot Black
Compiled by Reg Perrin

BRITISH BROADCASTING CORPORATION

Published by the British Broadcasting Corporation,
35 Marylebone High Street, London W1M 4AA
ISBN 0 563 20132 0
First published 1975
New revised edition 1983
© The British Broadcasting Corporation
and Joe Davis 1975, 1983
The Rules of Snooker © The Billiards
and Snooker Control Council

Diagrams by Designline

Filmset by August Filmsetting, Warrington, Cheshire
Printed in England by Hazell, Watson and Viney Ltd,
Aylesbury

The help of the following is gratefully acknowledged:
The Billiards and Snooker Control Council;
Powerglide Cues Ltd; Snooker Promotions Ltd;
Clive Everton, editor of *Snooker Scene*; Ted Lowe;
E.A. Clare & Son, Liverpool; Thomas Padmore &
Sons Ltd; The Composition Billiards Ball Supply Co
Ltd.
Joe Davis's 'How to Pot Black' is based on his own
book, *Complete Snooker for the Amateur*.
The cartoon on page 16 is reproduced by kind
permission of the *Daily Mail*. Other pictures
are reproduced as follows: pages 61, 65, 71, 73,75, 77,
79, 85, 89, 95, 99, 106, 113, 115, 117, 119, 123, 125,
127, 129, 137, 157, 160, 161, 163, 166, 172, 175 *left*
David Muscroft; 175 *right* John Carthy; 176 Tony
Workman; all other pictures are BBC copyright.
Cover picture taken at West Ealing Snooker Club by
Steve Benbow/Network.

Contents

Foreword

Many people still speak of snooker, and snooker on television, as a 'minority sport'. Yet during the concluding stages of the 1981 World Championship Final between Steve Davis and Doug Mountjoy fifteen million people were still watching at midnight on Easter Sunday.

Much of the credit for this phenomenal growth in popularity lies with those who devised and persevered with *Pot Black* from 1969 onwards. In truth, this annual sudden-death knock-out competition soon established itself as a highlight in the BBC-2 spring schedule. But in its wake followed a rapid growth in the number of people, particularly young people, who took an active interest in a game that so subtly blended skill with elegance and with style. This in turn seems bound to lead to an ever-increasing drive for perfection in play, leaving older, strictly amateur players – of which I am one – gasping with admiration on the sidelines.

So now the time has perhaps come to take notice of this new element in the snooker scene and give youth its own television chance, which we are doing with *Junior Pot Black*. Meantime to the senior professionals of the Pot Black scene we in the BBC would wish once again to say an annual 'thank you'.

Brian Wenham

Pot Black: The Game
by Reg Perrin

When Alex Higgins won the 1982 World Professional Snooker Championship his winner's cheque for £25,000 was the highest individual prize in the history of the game. The first World Championship had been instituted and won in 1927 by the late Joe Davis, who had persuaded the governing body of the day, the Billiards Association and Control Council, to approve such a competition, but their agreement contained the proviso that he should provide the trophy himself out of the attendance and entrance money. The silver cup that the 'Hurricane' lifted aloft in triumph in May 1982 was bought by Joe Davis in 1927 for £6 10 shillings!

Joe had begun his long and successful career as a billiards player but eventually realised that a greater potential public and commercial interest lay in the hardly considered game of snooker. Snooker had been born, if not out of contempt, certainly out of familiarity. Its great-grandfather, the game of billiards, had been played in various forms for over three hundred years, but billiards as we know it, using only three balls, had become for many repetitive and monotonous. A good player was able to score endless cannons by keeping the three balls closely bunched together. Games became never-ending with astronomical scores – the record was 499,315 (unfinished!) set up by Tom Reece in 1907 and took five weeks to achieve. Breaks of over 2000 are common and billiards, as a spectator sport, has gradually gone into a decline.

There are anachronistic references to billiards in Shakespeare's *Antony and Cleopatra* (Act 2 scene 5), but its origins are even earlier. It was developed over a considerable period of time via a game called 'paille maille', played in France in the fifteenth century. This was a form of croquet played with wooden balls and clubs. The popularity of the sport brought it to England during the Stuart period, and one of its venues in London gave rise to the name of the famous Pall Mall. The game was then 'miniaturised', becoming an indoor pastime, and was played on a special table using a 'mace' – the forerunner of today's cue. The mace, resembling a thin, blunt-ended hockey-stick, was used to push the balls through various hoops on the table – at this time there were no 'pockets'. (Even today the billiard tables in Europe are pocketless, and the French and Belgians play a game called 'Carambolage' where points are scored by cannons and making extensive use of the side cushions.)

In 1674 the *Complete Gamester* quoted billiards as being 'a most gentile, cleanly and ingenious game', but for over a century the game progressed only slowly until, in the 1820s, a London cabinet-maker, John Thurston, became intrigued with the game and gave it a new lease of life by completely revolutionising the design of the table. He replaced the wooden bed with slate, the stuffed cushions with india-rubber and the maces with thin, pointed cues. A French army officer, Captain Mingaud, invented a leather tip for the cue which, when applied with chalk, gave a higher degree of control on the cue-ball than had hitherto been possible, thus introducing the use of side, screw, stun, etc.

By 1852 'named' players were beginning to emerge. One of them, Edwin Kentfield, had in 1833 written his *Treatise on Billiards*, now a much sought-after collector's item. Tables became in demand overseas, especially where British troops were stationed. Which is where the story of snooker really begins! The *Radio Times* Television Supplement for 9 April 1937 stated: 'The origin of snooker is obscure, but the introduction of the game is attributed to Captain Snooker who was an officer in the Bengal Lancers in India.'

As far as is known today, 'Captain Snooker' never existed. There is now another and well-authenticated account of the game's origin. In the latter half of the nineteenth century variations on the theme of billiards included 'Pyramids', 'Pool' and 'Black Pool', where various coloured balls had been added to the traditional two whites and a red. In Jubbolpore, India, in 1875, a group of Army officers were playing Black Pool on the Mess billiards table when a young subaltern, Sir Neville Chamberlain, suggested the addition of other coloured balls with different scoring values. During the progress of this new game one of Sir Neville's opponents failed to pot a ball leaving Sir Neville with an unplayable shot. 'Gad sir, you're a regular snooker!' was the angry outburst from Sir Neville. (A snooker was the nickname for a first-year cadet at Woolwich Military Academy and obviously held in very low regard.) However, regaining his composure Sir Neville admitted that they were all 'snookers' at the game, and thus it was christened.

Before long, rumours of this new game of 'snooker' reached England and a well-known professional billiards player, John Roberts, travelled to India to learn about the game at first hand. He was introduced to Sir Neville Chamberlain in Calcutta by the Maharajah of Cooch Behar, the new rules were explained to him, and Roberts returned to England to demonstrate snooker to his colleagues. In 1891 John Dowland, another professional player, drew up the first set of recognised rules and the game became established in the UK. Colonel Sir Neville Chamberlain died on 28 May 1944 aged 88. His memories of having 'invented' snooker were related to the novelist, Sir Compton Mackenzie, and published in the *Billiard Player* in its April 1939 issue.

Although an Amateur Snooker Championship was instituted in 1916 and a few Regional Professional Championships had been played in the early 1920s, it was Joe Davis who was responsible both for the development of snooker as a spectator sport and for devising the techniques of play which are now taken for granted by today's professionals. Having established the first World Snooker Championship he won the event every year until 1946. It is somewhat surprising, therefore, that the first demonstration of snooker on BBC Television was given, in April 1937, not by Joe but by two of his contemporaries, Willie Smith and Horace Lindrum. Joe's début from the studios at Alexandra Palace was on 3 May 1937 when he and Tom Newman gave a ten-minute demonstration of billiards.

After Joe retired, undefeated, from World Championship play in 1947, he continued to play in lesser tournaments and exhibition matches, and in the early 1960s competed in several 'challenge' games on BBC TV's *Grandstand* (I had the pleasure of directing many of them). The first 147 maximum break to be eventually ratified as a world record was, once again, made by the great Joe at the Leicester Square Hall on 22 January

9

1955. He was now fifty-three and had been playing for thirty-five years, with a staggering total of 574 century breaks to his credit. He was awarded the OBE in 1963 for his services to charity and, when he finally retired from the game, in 1964, he vowed never to play again – not even in the privacy of his own billiards room. Nevertheless he maintained an active interest in the game in all its aspects as President of the Players' Association.

Pot Black, one of the early colour programmes on BBC-2, was first seen on 23 July 1969. From 1970 onwards Joe, having given the programme his approval, became an annual guest and presented the trophy to the *Pot Black* champions. In 1971 – despite his vow – he was even persuaded to take his cue from its dusty case and play some trick-shots! In 1976 the programme had the privilege of presenting Joe with the '*Pot Black* Personality Award' – a miniature trophy.

The eight players who competed in the first two *Pot Black* series in 1969–70 were Rex Williams, Ray Reardon, John Pulman, Jack Rea, Gary Owen, the late Kingsley Kennerley, John Spencer and Joe's 'younger' brother Fred. Thirteen other leading professionals have appeared in the series since then – David Taylor, Eddie Charlton, Alex Higgins, Graham Miles, Cliff Thorburn, Dennis Taylor, Willie Thorne, Perrie Mans, Doug Mountjoy, Jim Wych, Kirk Stevens, Terry Griffiths and Steve Davis.

Today the snooker industry is thriving both as a sport, where hundreds of youngsters take up the game each year, and as a commercial enterprise. The name of *Pot Black* has been used to christen snooker tables, cues, badges, snooker clubs, a magazine and, aptly enough, to advertise a certain well-known brand of Irish stout! Snooker writers and the Press have been unanimous in their verdict that television, and *Pot Black* in particular, have played a paramount role in dispelling the game's 'seedy' image of the past, creating instead a colourful shop-window for a game 'invented' by a group of Indian Army officers over a hundred years ago.

The table

An important ingredient in the *Pot Black* series is the table. Many viewers probably never think twice about it or, if they do, assume that the Snooker Table has not really altered in design or construction since the game was invented. But the Billiards Table, to give it its correct name, and its equipment have slowly evolved in construction and design over a very long period of time. (In Britain and the Commonwealth, there is now a tendency for players to call the tables 'Snooker Tables' and to purchase 'Snooker Cues', and even to ask for 'Snooker Chalk'.)

Whilst Britain plays the game of 'English billiards' and 'Snooker', most European countries play 'Carambolage' or 'Continental Billiards' – the principal difference being that the Continental-style tables do not have any pockets and the game is entirely made up of a series of cannons, while the English table has pockets at each corner and at the centre of each long side. (In the United States a large number of different games, all of which we generally refer to as 'American Pool', are played on tables which have pockets, but with a population of mixed European origin billiards follows the Continental style: tables without pockets.)

A full-sized billiard table is twelve foot long, six foot wide and about two foot ten inches high. The timbers most commonly used are mahogany, oak and walnut, and in the nineteenth century the bed of the table itself was also made of wood. In the second half of the nineteenth century tables manufactured in Liverpool had cast-iron underframes. These tables stood on six legs and one of them was in use in a staff canteen in Liverpool until a few years ago.

The actual 'bed' of the billiard table is now made of slate, although it was once made of iron. Such tables were to be found in Ireland at the beginning of this century, but obviously these 'iron beds' suffered from the damp atmosphere and would develop rust, thus staining the cloth. It was also very difficult to unscrew the nuts and bolts in order to move and reassemble a table. Experiments have recently been carried out with 'glass' beds, but there is still nothing better in sight than a slate bed. The advantages are that slate is easy to cut, to drill and to plane the surface; even in the course of wear, when small pieces may be chipped off the edges, it is reasonably easy to repair the damage using modern filler materials.

The first slate beds were introduced by John Thurston about 1834. The slates then were about one inch thick, but as time went on they became thicker and today a slate bed has to be two inches thick if it is going to be satisfactory. Each slab weighs between three and four hundredweight and requires four men to handle it. The total weight of a billiard table is therefore about one and three-quarter tons. So if you are toying with the idea of installing one in the lounge, make sure the floorboards are sound!

Table maintenance

Ensure that the table is brushed daily. This prevents dust and chalk-dust penetrating the cloth and forming uneven ridges on the slate. Brush the cushion cloths before the bed cloth. Always brush from baulk to spot end – along the nap of the cloth. Use a dust cover whenever the table is not in use, especially overnight.

After a period of six months or so the cloth should be removed so that dust and other particles can be cleaned off from the slate. At this time the cloth needs to be stretched, which will help prevent cue-damage. This will not only double the life of the cloth, but the balls will run faster and truer. When ironing, make sure that the iron is clean. Use a moderate heat – too hot an iron will discolour the cloth. As with brushing, ironing should be from the baulk to the top of the table and the iron should be lifted carefully at the end of the table to prevent damage to the cushions.

The cue

The original cue bore very little resemblance to the cue as it is today. The general shape was similar, as it was necessary to reach across the table in the same way as now. It had a normal cue-like shaft, but a wooden head, two to three inches wide and not unlike a small rake without the spikes, the balls being pushed or manoeuvred around the table. The name given to the 'cue' was a 'Mace'. Some mystery surrounds the evolvement of the modern-day cue, but it is generally thought that probably the first variation was to turn the mace shaft around and strike the ball with the thin end. Later a leather tip was added and finally the 'mace' head was discarded. Probably the only trace of the 'mace' in its modern counterpart is the flat on the butt end of the cue. During the Victorian period it was accepted that the cue could be turned around and placed on to the table, allowing the ball to be struck with the butt end. The ladies appeared to be the main culprits for this action, since it would have been unladylike to lean or stretch across the table.

The most important requirement for a first-class straight cue is high-quality timber, but in this modern age of mass production of all kinds of furniture for the home and industry this becomes progressively more difficult to obtain. The most popular timber for cues is sporting ash, coppice-grown and straight-grained. This sounds easy, but good-quality ash has to be tracked down and reserved. The importance of the specification has to be impressed on to the timber mill, since constant attention must be paid to the drying or moisture content of the material. If it is dried too fast the material will bend, making the manufacture of the cue far more difficult. On the other hand, if the moisture content is too high, it is most difficult to control the humidity loss, probably the most important reason for cues warping. If you extract the remaining moisture from any cue, it will bend like a bow; even bright lights or at least the heat that the lights generate will all help to dry out your cue.

The next most popular wood is 'Canadian maple', a good strong, sound timber with slightly less troublesome humidity factor, since the grain formation of maple is much closer, with less softwood between the grain (softwood acts like blotting paper and allows moisture to be added or extracted with ease). Maple is the most popular cue-wood in North America, where the stabilising of the moisture content is all-important in club rooms and houses that are constantly kept at temperatures in excess of 70°F. Needless to say, North America is probably the most difficult part of the world to keep cues in good condition.

Probably the most confusing point to a beginner is the choice of a cue with the ideal weight. From the manufacturer's point of view the ideal weight is probably about $16\frac{1}{2}$ to 17 ounces, as this means that very little extra weight has to be added into the butt of the cue. This can produce the cue of ideal balance, well forward. If the cue is supported on your index finger at approximately the points of the splice it should ideally tilt forward so that when cueing it will lie into the playing bridge. This does not of course mean that a cue with a balance well back cannot be played with effectively.

The main use of the ferrule (the brass collar at the top

end of the cue) is to avoid the cue shortening too quickly through constant retipping and levelling of the ferrule over the years (it is surprising how quickly this can happen). It also adds strength to a piece of timber that is, after all, only 10–11 mm thick, and could obviously quite easily split, as the power used on contact with the cue-ball is quite considerable. Tips are a constant worry to most players and the more competent the player the more worry they become. No two tips have the same playing quality: some are soft and spongy – not an ideal tip; some are very hard, which can be nearly as bad. A good tip can make the screw shot as easy as ABC.

Cues can go sticky, impregnated with a mixture of natural oils and dirt, and far too common a remedy for this is the use of sandpaper. Many a good cue is ruined by sandpapering, which removes both the artificial and the natural sealing agent, and once again allows the timber to dry out too quickly. The correct method is simple: a slightly dampened cloth rubbed up and down the shaft to remove any dirt and then a brisk rub with a clean dry cloth. This dries the cue thoroughly and produces a silky sheen that is a delight to handle.

The balls

The original billiard ball was made of ivory, and in the nineteenth century thousands of elephants were slaughtered to provide them. By 1890 nearly 15,000 cwt of ivory a year were passing through the Port of London and around 12,000 elephants a year were being killed for their tusks. On average, only four balls could be made from each tusk, and, as the density of the tusk varied considerably, only one or two of the four could be classed as top quality. To obtain a good set of billiard balls, therefore, might need seven or eight tusks.

An increasing demand for billiard balls and the growing scarcity of ivory led to experimentation with various substitutes. Peter Kinnear, a Scot who had emigrated to the United States in the 1860s and settled in Albany, about 150 miles from New York City, set to work to discover a substitute that would be cheaper and better than ivory. The problem was to find a suitable filler, and finally a friend called Hyatt, a chemist who subsequently invented the ball-bearing, discovered a perfect solution in the chemical, cellulose nitrate, now known as celluloid.

In 1868 the Albany Billiard Ball Company was formed and produced the Hyatt ball, which was sold towards the end of the century in England by the Bonzoline Manufacturing Co. Ltd under the name of 'Bonzoline'. In 1900 George Birt left the Albany Company and came to England, where with Percy Warnford-Davis he started to produce the crystalate ball, a composition ball with a cellulose nitrate base, very similar to the Hyatt ball In 1909 the Endolithic Company Ltd (who were marketing the crystalate ball) brought over from Australia the sensational young player George Gray, who made a series of the largest breaks ever made on a billiard table and established the reputation of the crystalate ball, after which it was adopted as the standard ball for all matches by the Billiards Association and Control Club.

Meanwhile a chemical firm in Germany was experimenting with the production of an entirely different type of ball with a phenol and formaldehyde base, the cast resin ball. It was rather lighter but had beautiful bright colours and a very attractive translucent appearance. The experiments were carried out by a brilliant German chemist, Dr Koebner, who in 1937 fled to London as a refugee. From then until his death twelve years later, he worked for the Billiard Ball Company, where a ball similar to the German product was perfected and marketed under the name 'vitalite'.

The cellulose nitrate type of ball was moulded from powder under great pressure and the resulting block of plastic material was turned and polished in a similar way to the old ivory ball, but the new cast resin ball was made by a much more modern and sophisticated process. The raw materials were mixed under heat in large stills until they produced a syrupy substance. This syrup was poured into glass flasks and then underwent a number of baking treatments lasting several days. Once again a hard block of plastic material was produced and had to be finished into a perfect sphere by means of a series of grinding and polishing operations on highly specialised machinery. The beautiful bright colours are obtained by adding aniline dyes during distillation.

However, for some years past it had been realised that the cellulose nitrate ball was becoming out of date as the raw materials became more difficult to obtain, and that the time had come to produce something better and more modern. After intensive experimentation, therefore, 'Super Crystalate' was put on the market in 1972. This ball has specially bright and attractive colours, is very hard and durable and its specific density is very similar to crystalate, or rather heavier than vitalite. It has been an instant success and has been adopted by the Billiards Association and is now exclusively used by the leading professionals. It is the ball used in *Pot Black*, where millions can see how well the balls respond to the players' skill.

'That's the sign of a great player—always chalks his cue before beating his opponent over the head with it.'

Pot Black: The Programme
by Jim Dumighan

A 'broadcasting phenomenon' was how one distinguished critic described *Pot Black*. The dictionary records a phenomenon as being an extraordinary happening; yet, in 1969, when the programme first appeared on BBC-2, mainly as an experiment to extend the potential of colour programmes, it certainly never occurred to anyone associated with it that it would quickly establish itself as a huge television success.

Reg Perrin, now the producer, recalls: 'We had a few mild reservations at the beginning. How would people react to the innovation of one-frame snooker? And would we ever be able to tempt an audience inside the studio to watch it?' Those mild reservations have long since evaporated, and without wishing to invite any charges of immodesty on our part, *Pot Black* is now internationally acclaimed as the biggest shop window ever in professional snooker.

We have often tried to analyse why this is so, and perhaps the simple explanation is that snooker is tailor-made for television. It is the one sport in which television illustrates perfectly the expertise of the top professional's technique in close-up. In cricket coverage, for example, you never see how a player uses his wrist in his bowling action or in his batting. But in snooker viewers can see the player's bridge hand and how he holds the cue. There is no gimmickry in *Pot Black* and perhaps it is the simplicity of it all which has motivated its success.

One elderly lady may well have got somewhere near the mark when she wrote: 'The programme is full of nice-mannered people with smart bow ties.' Bow ties and good manners apart, *Pot Black* is an established favourite with viewers in three continents. Besides the fanatical following in the United Kingdom, it has also taken off in New Zealand, Hong Kong and Australia, where the programme's impact has exceeded all expectations. Australian champion Eddie Charlton, *Pot Black* champion in 1972, 1973 and 1980, says: 'The programme is compulsive viewing in Australia. Each series has been shown within a few weeks after the UK transmissions. *Pot Black* players are hero-worshipped here.'

To the players who are invited to appear in it, *Pot Black* means much more than the occasional television engagement. It accords them overseas exposure, extra bookings and increased earning-power. The programme 'discovered' and nurtured two young players in Graham Miles and Dennis Taylor, both of whom claim *Pot Black* has had a considerable effect on their livelihoods and standings in the professional ranks.

Technical hiccups aside, the biggest problem surrounding any *Pot Black* recording session concerns the allocation of tickets for the studio audience. Approximately 1500 people visit the Pebble Mill studios in Birmingham each December – six sessions with a capacity of 250 – many of whom have waited patiently on the ticket list for up to nearly a year! There are many more than 1500 disappointed fans whose written applications have been received after the list has been closed – nowadays by the end of March.

The first *Pot Black* competition ran for eight weeks and featured eight players in an 'instant death' knockout competition. From 1970 onwards the series was extended to sixteen weeks and each series up to 1976 contained six or eight professionals. Various permutations have been employed to arrive at the required sixteen programmes, ensuring at the same time that both the viewer and the player understood the system!

It is not possible with eight players for them all to play each other even once, in sixteen weeks. Initially it would take twenty-eight weeks for this to happen. Four *Pot Black* Champions against four Challengers in two leagues has worked well, at least mathematically. This method was used in 1975 and 1976 and provided a *Pot Black* 'Champion' against a 'Challenger' in the Finals. (The runner-up in each year was Dennis Taylor.) Also in each competition there is a prize for the highest break of the series and since 1976 a special award – a replica of the *Pot Black* Trophy – has been presented to snooker personalities during the final ceremonies.

The 1977 series featured twelve players and included the first appearance of the left-handed South African,

Perrie Mans, and the Welshman, Doug Mountjoy. Mans was the reigning South African champion whereas Mountjoy had just turned professional after winning the World Amateur Championship in Mans' home town of Johannesburg. Coincidentally, it was these two players who found themselves competing in the final, with Mans earning the title of *Pot Black* Champion 1977.

The programme celebrated its tenth birthday in 1978 and by the end of the fifteen-week series, won by Doug Mountjoy in a three-frame Final from Graham Miles, it had amassed an average viewing figure of three million viewers each week!

In 1979, the team of eight players included all six previous winners of the Trophy. Ray Reardon, the first *Pot Black* champion in 1969, won for the second time, against Doug Mountjoy in the three-frame Final. In the closing ceremonies, the actor Sir Ralph Richardson presented the Trophy, and a special prize – a decanter which had belonged to Joe Davis – was presented by his widow June for the highest break in the series.

Pot Black entered the eighties with another strong team of eight professionals: Ray Reardon, Doug Mountjoy, Dennis Taylor, Graham Miles, John Spencer, Perrie Mans, Eddie Charlton and the 1979 World Snooker Champion, Terry Griffiths. Reardon's attempt to win the Trophy for the third time failed when he was beaten in the three-frame Final by the Australian, Eddie Charlton. The main prizes were presented by Cliff Morgan, OBE, the Head of BBC Outside Broadcasts Group, Television, and June Davis presented the Joe Davis Trophy to Dennis Taylor for his break of 87, the highest in the series. A delighted and very surprised Alan Weeks opened the envelope containing the name of the winner of the 'Personality Award' – to discover that he himself was the recipient!

The selection of the eight players for 1981 was based on the quarter-finalists in the 1980 World Snooker Championships. Among them were two young Canadians, Kirk Stevens and Jim Wych, and the reigning World Champion, also from Canada, Cliff Thorburn, who competed with Ray Reardon, David Taylor, Alex Higgins, Eddie Charlton and Steve Davis.

For the first time in many years Sydney Lee, the programme's famous referee, was (due to ill-health) unable to officiate, and John Williams from Wrexham, the 'senior' referee, was invited to take over Syd's duties. The competition was dominated by the Canadians – the winner was Cliff Thorburn, the runner-up Jim Wych, and Kirk Stevens won the highest break prize with a score of 79. *Pot Black*'s 'Personality Award' also went overseas – to Australia's Eddie Charlton. George Howard, Chairman of the BBC, presented the main prizes after a Final watched by over nine million viewers.

The 1982 series was notable on at least two not entirely unrelated counts: audience figures – an average of over eight million viewers a week was the largest in the programme's history; and the presence of the 1981 World Champion, Steve Davis, who, although he had previously played in the 1979 and 1981 series, had really captured the public's imagination by 1982. The Final featured the youngest and the oldest of the eight competitors, Steve Davis and Eddie Charlton, with Steve gaining his first *Pot Black* Championship by two frames to nil. The presentations were made by the Minister for Sport, Neil Macfarlane MP. Eddie Charlton, the runner-up, also won

Pot Black *Final 1982. Neil Macfarlane MP, the Minister for Sport, makes the presentation to Steve Davis. Alan Weeks is on the right.*

the highest break prize with a score of 98. The two losing semi-finalists were Cliff Thorburn and Doug Mountjoy, and the 'non-qualifiers' were David Taylor, Dennis Taylor, Alex Higgins and Ray Reardon, who also won the 'Personality Award'.

Those taking part in the 1983 *Pot Black* series will be Eddie Charlton, Steve Davis, Alex Higgins, Tony Knowles, Ray Reardon, Kirk Stevens, Willie Thorne and Jimmy White.

Pot Black honours list

1969   Winner: Ray Reardon 88 – 29
       Runner-up: John Spencer
       Highest break in series: Ray Reardon (99)

1970   Winner: John Spencer 88 – 27
       Runner-up: Ray Reardon
       Highest break in series: Fred Davis (54)

1971   Winner: John Spencer 61 – 40
       Runner-up: Fred Davis
       Highest break in series: Fred Davis (73)

1972   Winner: Eddie Charlton 75 – 43
Runner-up: Ray Reardon
Highest break in series: John Spencer (66)

1973   Winner: Eddie Charlton 93 – 33
Runner-up: Rex Williams
Highest break in series: Eddie Charlton (110)

1974   Winner: Graham Miles 77 – 37, 70 – 49
Runner-up: John Spencer
Highest break in series: Graham Miles (68)

1975   Winner: Graham Miles 81 – 27
Runner-up: Dennis Taylor
Highest break in series: Fred Davis (87)

1976   Winner: John Spencer 69 – 42
Runner-up: Dennis Taylor
Highest break in series: Eddie Charlton (64)

1977   Winner: Perrie Mans 90 – 21
Runner-up: Doug Mountjoy
Highest break in series: Perrie Mans (59)

1978   Winner: Doug Mountjoy 43 – 55, 97 – 23,
111 – 16
Runner-up: Graham Miles
Highest break in series: Doug Mountjoy (101)

1979   Winner: Ray Reardon 79 – 51, 25 – 82, 84 – 41
Runner-up: Doug Mountjoy
Highest break in series: Doug Mountjoy (82)

1980   Winner: Eddie Charlton 16 – 74, 85 – 30,
68 – 54
Runner-up: Ray Reardon
Highest break in series: Dennis Taylor (87)

1981   Winner: Cliff Thorburn 68 – 39, 85 – 50
Runner-up: Jim Wych
Highest break in series: Kirk Stevens (79)

1982   Winner: Steve Davis 82 – 40, 85 – 38
Runner-up: Eddie Charlton
Highest break in series: Eddie Charltòn (98)

How to Pot Black
by the late Joe Davis

Joe Davis presents the Pot Black *trophy to the 1975 winner Graham Miles. Alan Weeks is in the middle.*

Joe Davis was born at Whitwell, Derbyshire, on 15 April 1901, and began playing billiards at the age of ten. He was World Billiards Champion 1928–33, and undefeated World's Snooker Champion 1927–46, when a weak right eye forced him to retire from Championship play. He scored the maximum break of 147 on 22 January 1955 at the Leicester Square Hall. This was eventually ratified as a new World Record, beating his previous best of 146.

In the 1920s, when other players were treating snooker lightly, Joe Davis saw its possibilities and concentrated on fundamental principles which became the standard professional techniques of today. Joe's last appearance in public was at the Crucible Theatre, Sheffield, watching his brother Fred play in the 1978 World Championship.

He was taken ill and returned to London, undergoing a serious operation. Although he made a brief recovery the strain of that and previous operations proved too much. Joe's death was announced on 10 July 1978 – he was seventy-seven.

Joe Davis's influence on snooker cannot be over-estimated. He leaves a legacy for all players with these secrets of his success.

Get your own cue

You should have your own cue, look after it, and use no other. A cue has weight, balance, thickness and power. The ideal weight for snooker is $16\frac{1}{2}$ ounces. With this weight power, screw and stun shots can be made with a slower rhythm and shorter action than with a lighter cue. A cue should have balance. Avoid the cue which is abnormally thick at the butt end, or which tapers down so much that a very small tip has to be used. It should be shorter than most billiard cues – slightly less than shoulder height. In general it should look and be fairly powerful. The tip end should be of medium size – $10\frac{1}{2}$–11 millimetres – and the butt should fit comfortably into your hand.

The tip is perhaps most important of all. If you look at a row of cues standing in the rack of any club you will find them of all shapes and sizes. Some are rounded, some are flat; some are very soft, others are extremely hard. The ideal tip – it may be difficult to find – is springy and holding so that it can bite on the ball. It also has plenty of resistance so that the power goes through. The tip should be like the cue itself, resilient but built for power. Only an expert can fit a tip. If your own tip is unsatisfactory tell him exactly what you want in replacing it.

Learn to pot first

It is an obvious fact that if you can't pot, you can't play snooker. Some people seem to be born good potters. Have they got what is known as 'a good eye'? Definitely not – you don't need 'a good eye' in that sense for snooker. (For a moving ball, yes, since it enables you to time and gauge the flight of the ball.) If a man is a good potter, the chances are that he has a good cue action. Until you can pot really well, you have no hope of constructing the big breaks that win. Break-building requires two-ball control; you have to pot your ball – that is one-ball control; and you also have to place the cue-ball for the next stroke – that is two-ball control. Until and unless the pot is automatic, needing only a small part of your concentration, control of the cue-ball is impossible.

The stance
The fundamental of playing snooker is that there should be absolutely no movement whatever of any part of the body except the striking arm.

In general terms, my stance is much like a boxer. The feet are a comfortable distance apart to enable you to get right down with your chin on the cue without bending the knee of your back leg.

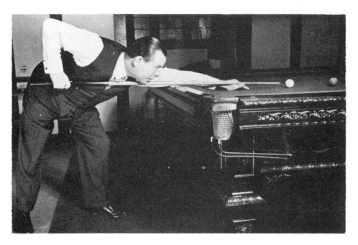

The weight is forward – that is, leaning slightly on the forward leg. The back leg is the bracer – the anchor; it must never in any circumstances move until the stroke is complete. Rising on to the toe of the back foot in making the stroke is a common fault, and you must eliminate it at once. The front leg is bent, but the knee should not sag outward, which is another common fault. If it does sag outward, the whole body is liable to sway sideways. The front knee must point in the direction of the stroke. In fact, it helps to keep the cue going along that line. Make it do so! The toe of the front foot should also go straight ahead, or as nearly so as is possible with comfort. Avoid any sign of discomfort in this stance: comfort is a first essential.

Summary

1 Weight forward.
2 Rear leg braced rigid.
3 Front knee bent, taking the weight.

Common faults

1 Both knees bent.
2 Legs spread sideways instead of in line with stroke.
3 Weight on haunches, instead of forward.
4 Front knee sagging outwards.
5 Legs too far apart or too close together.
6 Habit of rising on rear toe when striking.

The head

Practically all body movement comes either from the legs or the head, and the aim is to eliminate all movement on the stroke. I firmly believe in getting the chin down to the level of the cue. It is like sighting with a rifle: the nearer the eye is to the actual line of the stroke the more accurate the stroke is likely to be.

During the movement of the cue the head must not move, and this includes the eyes. Ideally the head should remain completely still until the object-ball is in the pocket. On impact, the eyes should be looking at the exact point on the object-ball where contact is intended: you must resist all temptation to look towards the pocket. Following the object-ball with the eyes means more often than not that the eyes get to the pocket before the ball does. That means anticipatory head movements and the head must be kept still at all costs.

Don't let yourself be persuaded that you are carrying stillness to unnecessary extremes. You cannot err in keeping the head down too long. The penalty is failure, almost every time.

Summary

1 Get the chin right down to cue level.
2 Keep the head down and still until the ball is in the pocket.
3 Avoid eye-swivel.

Common faults

1 Head too far above cue.
2 Jerking up of head on the stroke.
3 Allowing the eyes to follow or precede the object-ball.

The bridge

With the feet, the bridge forms the tripod, and must be regarded as the point of pinning down the whole body. Move it during the action, and you are doomed to failure. In this respect it is like the left elbow which supports a rifle; the slightest movement will throw the shot off target. Making a firm bridge at snooker, however, is much easier than keeping a steady forearm for a rifle.

I have found that the great majority of players make a very poor bridge, perhaps unaware of its importance. Even among good players there is sometimes a slight movement in the bridge hand. This must affect the line of stroke.

The correct way to make a normal bridge with the hand on the table is as follows: having decided on your stroke, aligned your body and placed your feet, get down to it, stretch the left arm and place the left hand on the table with all fingers splayed as wide as possible. Draw the fingers inwards, keeping them taut and unbent. Grip the

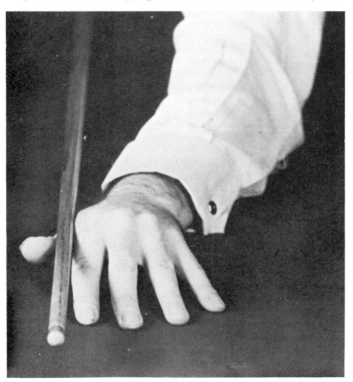

cloth hard with the pads of the fingers, and cock the thumb. You should have a bridge almost literally fastened to the table, and a smooth channel for the cue to slide through.

The arm should be straight, thrust out from the shoulder as far as it will go. You should feel a line of tension running from the left hand through the left arm and shoulders right down to the right elbow. With that tension you will be assured of a well-braced upper stance and you will find that the striking arm hangs loosely from the elbow, swinging easily and independently without affecting the rigidity of the upper arm. This is exactly as it should be for the correct slide of the cue.

Summary
1 A firm, unshakeable bridge.
2 Bridge arm straight and taut.
3 Brace back the shoulder of the cue arm.

Common faults
1 Bridge-fingers bunched together.
2 No grip on the cloth with bridge-fingers.
3 Thumb badly cocked.
4 Elbow of bridge-arm loose and bent.
5 Cueing – shoulder too far forward.

Cue hold
You cannot play power shots consistently well unless you have a firm hold – not a clutch, remember. The cue should

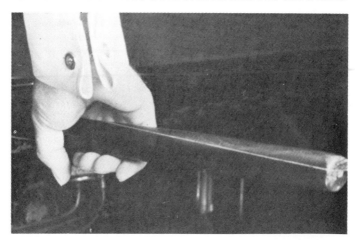

rest on the pads of the middle joints of all four fingers, while the grip is made with the thumb and the first two fingers only. Avoid tension in the finger and arm muscles, but avoid a floppy wrist. Tension will ruin the action and the floppy wrist merely increases the probability of error. You can assess the degree of firmness needed in the grip by putting a cue on the table and picking it up by the butt with the right hand. The pressure you need for taking the weight is roughly the pressure you should use to hold the cue.

The action

I can best describe the movement of the cue as similar to a piston – dead-straight and horizontal, moving rhythmically in its well-oiled channel. The 'casing' is the whole body and limbs except the right forearm. The piston is the cue, and the wrist and forearm are the connecting rods. Nothing else moves until the stroke is advanced when the upper part of the cue-arm is drawn down by the forward movement. The body is bolted down at three points – the back foot, the bridge and the head.

Striking the cue-ball just where you want and intend to strike it is perhaps the most difficult thing in the whole game. It is certainly the most important. The cue must remain practically horizontal all the way through the stroke. It is important therefore to maintain a flat action, and to avoid any lateral movement, whether at the bridge or the butt. If the cue is swinging sideways the chances are that you will not push it along the line of aim: and even if you do, you will probably apply side without meaning to and the ball will be pulled off its course.

Remember – a flat, horizontal cue-slide with no lateral deviation – the piston action.

Forearm movement

As I said earlier, you need a straight left arm, the right shoulder braced back from the chest, and a line of tension running from the bridge itself up the left arm, through to the right shoulder, and down as far as the right elbow. Owing to the position of the shoulders that line is not actually a straight line. The straight line is made by the ball, the cue and the right upper-arm.

The cue is held a few inches from the end of the butt. The exact distance depends on the length and balance of the cue as well as the type of stroke. Different players have different preferences. But, wherever the grip is, see that the forearm drops vertically. On the backward movement the forearm moves freely as though on a hinge. (The tendency among many amateurs is for the cue to be held nearer the butt end so that the forearm is not vertical but angled backwards.)

The hinge
This movement must be carefully mastered. The common fault here is to swing the cue from the shoulder, thus getting a stiffness right down the arm. The result of this is lack of power and a pump-handle action. I find that my ties become frayed by the constant rubbing of the cue, and always in the same place. With the cue brushing the tie you will find that the cue is running nicely underneath the body, which gives you a feeling of control and straight shooting.

Get your stance and bridge properly lined up, make sure that the right elbow is dead behind the line of cue, and swing the cue freely from the elbow. Check up on the forearm – is it dead vertical? Is the cue running under the body and against the tie? Is it running horizontally? Have you braced the shoulder?

I feel confident that, by the adoption of the stance alone, you must have improved your game already. By adopting the cue action you may not improve at once, and you may be tempted to fall back into your own style. But persist with the theory of verticals and horizontals and it will not be long before results come along.

Summary
1 Hold the cue firmly, resting on the pads of the fingers, but gripped by the thumb and first two fingers.
2 Right elbow dead behind the line of the cue.
3 Right forearm swinging from the elbow hinge.
4 Right forearm dropping vertically.
5 Piston action – true horizontal.
6 Cue brushing the tie.

The travel
Some favour a very long bridge – as much as eighteen inches. Too long a bridge results in loss of control and sloppiness of cue action, and too short a bridge causes

chronic cramp in the movement. My own distance is roughly a foot, if anything slightly more. I find that the backward part of the action benefits from as short a distance as possible. The more I cut it down, the more control I had over direction, and potting became more accurate.

I eventually settled on five inches as the shortest backswing commensurate with smooth action. Having cut the backswing to a workable minimum, the movement *after* contact calls for just the reverse treatment. The follow-through has, if anything, to be lengthened. It eliminates the stab and jerk; it gives rhythm and timing; and it fights against the 'flourish', which is a bad habit of many players. So there you have the lesson – see that you have a very good follow-through. This applies to practically every shot on the table, including the screw.

Summary

1 Length of bridge – twelve to fifteen inches from bridge-hand to cue-tip.
2 Short hand movement.
3 Consistent follow-through.
4 Keep the flat, horizontal piston-like action throughout, particularly in the finish of the stroke.

The driving action

Cue-action is not a swing, neither is it a push. Yet it is far more of a push than a swing inasmuch as the hand does shove the cue along the piston groove in a very deliberate way. I think the best description is a *drive*. When I come to make the stroke I take the cue back slower and then make a slight pause before deliberately thrusting it forward. This deliberateness, plus the horizontal action, combine to give the feel of the drive.

I think the bowing arm of a violinist is very much like the ideal cue action. There is flexibility in the fingers and at the wrist-joint; but the fingers do not move without the wrist and the wrist does not act without the forearm. The violinist's wrist is somewhat more fluent but the fingers, wrist and forearm are all of one piece and it is really the forearm which creates the main propelling force. Let me ask you to carry a mental picture of a controlled, delayed, deliberate movement (not a swing), so that when you face up to the stroke you are concentrating on that sort of

stroke. This type of driving action makes the follow-through automatic and gives control against flourishes, jerks and most other evils. Make a pause before the forward drive. This will give you time to secure complete control over the cue. It prevents 'head-up', slashing, bad finishing and many other faults. It brings better potting and enables one to gauge the pace of the cue-ball.

Speed comes from the action and from follow-through. It does not come entirely from the speed of the cue or from a longer action. The fact that more power is applied means a greater need for control over direction. So, in playing a power shot it is even more vital to pause for control before making the forward drive. This is one of my most treasured 'secrets' and it is up to you to make the most of it.

Contact

Only a professional, and high-class one at that, regularly hits the cue-ball where he means to hit it. If you intend to make a plain-ball stroke – that is, striking dead centre – and the object ball is three feet or more from the cue-ball, any side you accidentally apply will carry the cue-ball off its line and rob you of the pot. Side is spin, and a side-spinning ball cannot travel straight. If you want to stun the cue-ball, you aim below the centre, and of course if the point of contact is higher, you don't stun your ball. The horizontal groove will go a long way to help you connect accurately with the cue-ball. Practice will go much further. It is always necessary to concentrate on this matter right up to the start of the action. If accurate striking does not become automatic, it won't be there at all!

Finding the angle

Snooker and billiards just cannot be worked out by Euclid or a protractor. Very often, and especially at short range, the mathematical angle is near enough right, and the ball goes down. In any case it is always some sort of guide and will take you near the pocket if not in. But it is not the true potting angle.

I believe there is only one absolutely certain way of mastering the angle – it consists of experiment and memory. By now your cue action ought to be reliable, and having selected your angle you ought to be able to put the object-ball along the line which is right according to your estimate of the angle.

Place the object-ball on the pink spot and the cue-ball near the top cushion so that it is not quite in line with the pink and a baulk-pocket. Now study the angle for potting in the baulk-pocket. Then try to pot it. If you miss, register on which side of the pocket you missed and by how much. I expect that in three successive attempts you will miss the pocket on the same side by roughly the same margin. Having proved to yourself that your judgement was wrong, you can now alter the angle – even if it does not look right – and when you pot the ball, memorise the lesson you have taught yourself. There is only one thing to do with angles that beat you: register results until you know on which side your judgement is wrong. Then experiment until you find the correct angle and remember it for all time.

Eye on which ball?

At the moment of striking the eyes should be on the object-ball. Moreover, they should be concentrated on that section of the object-ball giving the angle of pot. But it is just as easy to fail through incorrect striking of the cue-ball as through reaching an incorrect angle on the object-ball. My own procedure is this: before getting down to it, I have aligned my body. With the cue I sight again and change my feet if necessary. Then I make sure that I am aiming to strike the cue-ball where I want to strike it. Then I confirm my line by shifting my eyes to the object-ball. Before I make the stroke, my eyes come back for one last quick look at the cue-ball, to ensure that I hit it where I want to. When the cue starts to move, my eyes are on the object-ball and there they stay, controlling my head. That last quick look is invaluable, and I believe this feature will give immediate improvement to any player. It is not difficult to incorporate in your style, but it must not be overdone or prolonged.

Never let your eyes wander towards the pocket! The magnetic attraction of the pocket passes from the brain to the hand and is responsible for that pulling away of the cue which causes incorrect impact on the cue-ball and over-cutting of the angle on the object ball. There is nothing whatever to be gained by trying to look at the pocket and the object-ball at the same time, since you have determined your angle. On the other hand, there is everything to be lost.

Here is my final word on the art of potting: having made up your mind to pot a ball, be wholehearted and single-minded about the job. Don't allow yourself any fears of failure. Don't be obsessed by what you may leave on. And don't tell yourself that this is a pot you usually miss or that it is a very difficult shot. *Attack the ball.*

Using the rest

In using the ordinary rest, it is important to get the head of the rest properly positioned. Most players place it too far away from the cue-ball. The distance should not be more than twelve inches, even though the cue cannot run horizontally. The shaft of the rest is held firmly down on the table. The grip of fingers and thumb is moderate – neither too firm nor too light. I find the best sighting line is from the point of the chin. The end of the butt is three inches or so below the chin and you will find that you will be helped a good deal by looking down the line of the cue to see that it is travelling along a line below the chin, and not to one side or the other. Follow-through is both important and simple.

Avoid raising the cue-butt too high – a downward action adds to the complication by creating spin – and avoid complicated strokes with the rest. Don't add to your troubles unless it is within your capacity to do so. It is a simple matter to stun a ball when using the rest, especially if the pot is easy; but it is asking for trouble to attempt a screw-shot when already over-reaching to hit the ball.

The spider, used for positions where ordinary bridging is impossible, needs delicate placing. The best plan is to take up the spider near the head and, getting close to the cue-ball, place the whole rest in position on the table. When this is possible, it saves all that awkward operation of suspending the head of the spider over a cluster of balls, or working it in between from a distance of four feet. It's very easy to foul with a spider before you have a chance to do so with your shot!

Since the bridge of the spider is high, the stroke must be somewhat downward and more often than not there is only the top part of the cue-ball to hit. In these cases the intention should be to play into the ball. Don't play a hurried, skidding blow. In all awkward strokes the one great secret is to get so comfortable that you can play at leisure – a calculated, well-timed stroke. Never try any

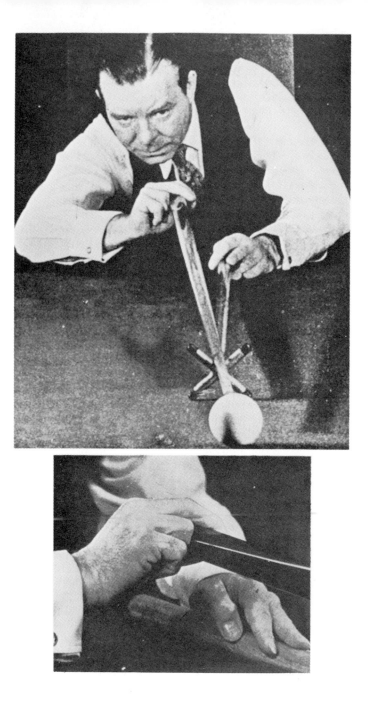

funny stuff. Be satisfied to pot your ball or leave nothing. Never attempt anything at less than medium pace; never attempt side or stun. Just get the ball in the hole and be content. (The half-butts are useful as punting poles but, on a twelve-foot billiard table which calls for accuracy, they are rough-and-ready instruments and nothing more.)

Screw and stun

There is no mystery about break-building at snooker. It is simply a combination of certain strokes. To make sizeable breaks regularly you must have potting skill and the mastery of certain strokes which will gain you position for the next ball. Stun or screw gives much more exact control and one can keep the cue-ball around the pyramid and the black spot as long as there are reds to pot, thus securing the highest possible value for each shot.

In any scoring stroke your first duty is to pot the ball. It is much more important to pot it, without good position, than to risk missing it while making the cue-ball position certain. There are often occasions when a plain-ball stroke – one which is struck slightly above centre, and with no spin of any kind – is the correct one to play. From such a stroke the cue-ball always takes a certain amount of 'throw' after striking the object-ball. The maximum throw normally is an angle of about forty-five degrees, made at half-ball contact. But by striking the ball with great force an additional amount of bounce is added to the geometrical angle. You can therefore exceed the forty-five degrees maximum by adding the bounce of a forcing plain stroke.

It is a good thing to study every stroke you play, as well as every stroke your opponent plays. It has the double advantage of giving you information and of keeping your mind in a calm reflective mood.

What complicates the study of cue-ball paths is the reverse angles taken by cushion contact. One often sees a player pot the black and watch his ball as it comes back off the side cushion into the middle pocket!

Stun-screw group

This group of strokes consists of the application of reverse spin. By striking the ball above centre, top spin is applied, giving the ball an extra forward-rotating movement. By striking the ball below centre, it is given reverse spin, so that, although the ball is travelling forward, the bottom or reverse spin is causing it to rotate backwards as it goes forward.

At cricket the bowler applies spin by twisting the ball with his fingers or wrist as he delivers it. To apply spin to a snooker ball, you need a good cue-tip, resilient and equally weighted snooker balls, and a cloth in good condition – the newer and the heavier the better. You may not be able to change your table or the set of balls upon it – but you can keep your cue reasonably well tipped and chalked. Remember that your object is to spin the ball and that the cloth is your 'turf'.

Screw is not obtained by power or speed. The whole secret lies in making the cue-tip give that undercutting spin by taking a grip on the ball's skin, just as the spin bowler does on the cricket ball. Plain striking will not do this, even though the right point is struck. The action for screw-stun is shorter than normal on the backward run, and this will tempt you to jerk or snatch, which is fatal. The ideal tempo is smooth and rhythmic – exactly as in the normal plain-ball stroke, up to the moment of impact. You are now playing a stroke calling for extra skill and concentration, and the natural tendency is to make long preparations and then a hurried stroke. That results in stabbing or jerking. A good stance, with freedom and independence in the cue-arm, will help you a lot to preserve the rhythm. The bridge must be lowered and the cue horizontal.

At the moment of impact the spin is applied. This is done by a short snappy action which makes the tip bite the ball. You follow through, but you do not swing through, and when the tip goes through it must grip the ball. Try, on impact, to take a distinctly stronger hold on the cue without checking the action. This applies the 'nip'. You have to 'feel' the screw as you apply it. Unless there is a danger of the cue-ball coming back suddenly – and it frequently does – hold on long enough to ensure that the direction of the cue is perfect.

Summary

1 Make sure, whatever happens, of potting your ball.
2 Screw is the application of reverse spin.
3 A holding but firm cue-tip is essential.

4 Extra force may make for inaccuracy.
5 The cue action is shorter – snappy – tighten the grip on contact. The cue follows through.
6 You must feel the tip holding on to and spinning the ball.
7 The cue-ball must be struck low.
8 The bridge must be lowered, the butt must not be raised and the action must retain the horizontal.
9 The bridge is lowered by turning the hand over onto the pad at the base of the thumb. Do not lower the knuckles.
10 Play into the ball so that the cue-tip grips and spins it.

Use of 'side'

If you are in the early stages of learning to play good snooker, I would advise you not to use 'side'. To a proficient player its use can be a source of great satisfaction, especially in positional play, but no matter how good a player you are, I would strongly recommend the use of side only when the cue-ball has to carry a relatively short distance.

There is the same instinctive fear of miscueing when using side as when using screw, and for that reason a large number of players do not apply the maximum. It will help the stroke, as well as intensify the spin, if the cue-ball is struck low. The line of aim is through one side of the ball, so the whole of the stance must be taken up along that line.

Before letting the cue go take one final look at the point of aim.

The power drive

You may well believe that a professional at a big snooker match is 'putting on an act' when he uses a power drive – that is, a stroke needing maximum force. No professional plays this kind of stroke merely for effect. It is a most hazardous and dangerous stroke: and where is the effect if one misses the pot?

The longer back-swing tends to alter the path of the cue and the greater speed of the forearm is likely to create movement throughout the right shoulder and side. It is this second factor which is the chief problem, since the cue wanders from its groove, the tip does not make contact on the cue-ball where it was intended (hence frequent miscued strokes), and the whole line of the cue is altered, which results in missing the pot.

There is no golden secret for the power drive. If there were, all professionals would have learned it and made themselves proficient. My advice therefore is largely a series of 'don'ts':

Don't hit too hard. By striking above centre, you will add impetus by applying a forward-rotating spin. By timing your blow, you will gain the maximum amount of forward spin and it will help you to strike the cue-ball really accurately.

Don't use the power drive unless the cue-ball is quite close to the object-ball – about eighteen inches. Even two feet between balls is too far if the object-ball has any considerable distance to travel to the pocket.

Never use it except for positional strokes.

Don't overdo the grip on the butt of the cue or you will set up a tension in the forearm, affecting the cue-travel. A good follow-through is essential. It will help to apply and it will help to keep the cue on its true path.

Make sure first of the pot – more power-drive 'sitters' are missed than all other sitters put together!

The swerve

This is a very useful stroke to get one out of a snooker. Only rarely, however, can you expect to do more than just hit the object-ball. The effect is gained by applying a considerable amount of spin. Instead of being straight, the course of the ball is bent into the shape of an arc. The outward part of the arc is shorter than the inward part: how much shorter depends upon the sharpness of the curve and the speed of the ball.

As height is wanted here, your bridge must be raised. The bridge consists of the pads of the four fingers pressed firmly, while the thumb is cocked high. The butt is raised to an angle of about forty-five degrees or half-way to vertical. I can best describe the blow itself as snappy, pinched, as though driving the ball into the table, and there is· practically no follow-through. The stroke is therefore a downward one, aimed at below centre. Contact on the ball must be hard, as though moving a ball six times the weight. Not a push – feel the tip bite into the ball. Don't play too hard, otherwise the ball will not have time to complete its arc – it won't come back!

The higher you raise the butt of the cue, the more spin you apply. This you can only judge by experience. The job is to control the amount of swerve. Steadiness is important, because of the minimum of stability in the bridge.

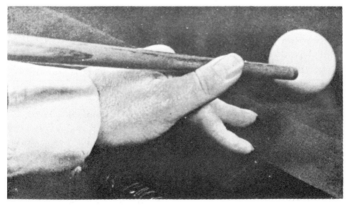

Applying spin

The art of doubling

HHDoubling is a very important stroke, one of tremendous assistance in the building of breaks and in which great accuracy is to be obtained both in potting and in the control of the cue-ball for subsequent position. Do not despise the double. On the contrary, when there is nothing else on, study the possibility of a double before deciding whether a safety stroke will have to be played.

The correct angle for point of contact for a double cannot be taught. The angle of incidence equals the angle of reflection; and that is really your only guide. Going to the intended pocket and looking at the shot backwards is often very helpful.

The habit of playing doubles with terrific force is bad. Force is not only unnecessary but is likely to result in the cue moving from its proper line. Cushions cannot often return to normal quickly enough when a ball is banged in at great speed, and the result is that the ball tends to bury itself in the cusion and come off at the wrong angle.

During a big break – which I hope you will soon be making – it is almost inevitable that you are faced with having to finish or pot a ball standing against, or very near to, a side cushion. The only chance is to double it, usually into a centre pocket. If, at this stage, it is going to be a double or nothing, play the preceding stroke for position on the double. A player's cue action, provided he is not one of those hard hitters, is generally better when playing a double than on an ordinary pot. This is because he is not aiming to cut or drive the ball into a pocket in his line of vision, and consequently he feels no tendency to pull the cue off its line. Concentrate on the position of the cue-ball for the next stroke. Nothing is more disappointing than to bring off a nice double, only to find that no colour is 'on' after all.

Plants or sets

All experienced players constantly watch the changing positions of the balls, especially to spot a 'plant', or 'set' as some call it, as soon as it appears. They hope their opponent will not see it, or will not have the opportunity to use it. A plant is regarded as a stone certainty, yet the playing of it gives much pleasure to the striker.

The plant position consists of two object-balls which are touching and standing in a straight line (drawn through their centres to a pocket). The general belief is that if the first of these object-balls is struck, then the second is bound to enter the pocket. Dead plants are regarded as unmissable, but now and then the player gets a shock when the second object-ball does not go down. Don't imagine that plants are not missable. They are, if you take them for granted. Unless the nearest object-ball is struck correctly, the plant is always liable to fail, and more especially if the planted ball has a few feet to travel. Play full back on to the first of two touching balls and the second will fly straight ahead every time. But when the contact is made at an angle away from the dead-straight line, a squeeze takes place between the three balls, causing the second object-ball to be pushed off its normal line. Striking at the correct potting-angle is, of course, equivalent to playing full ball, in that the first object-ball gives the second a kick in the direct line of the plant. Strike at a different angle, and the blow is no longer through the centres. Thus the squeeze takes place and the second object-ball is deflected to one side or other of the line of plant.

The moral of all this is that plants are never to be taken for granted. They are to be played at the correct potting angle; otherwise they may go wrong.

Non-touching plants
Planting one ball on to another when the two object-balls are some little distance apart is a very difficult type of stroke, as well as being the most fascinating and satisfying of all forms of potting. Such a stroke is always worth trying if nothing else is 'on', particularly when there is no more than an inch or two between the object-balls. Judgement must be minutely exact, however. Some players are fond of shaping at the first object-ball as though to pot the second with it, in order to see more clearly the angle for that part of the stroke. At times, it is necessary to do this. One learns in various ways about the intricacies of the game by such experiments.

Conclusion
I have come to the conclusion that nothing ever said about this game should be accepted without personal experiment and proof. It seems that you can prove almost anything by mathematics and drawing and equalising

angles, but that when you apply these theories to a set of composition balls on a piece of West of England cloth, the mathematical results simply do not turn up. Instead, something else happens with such monotonous regularity that it is clear there is some other factor not reckoned with.

No doubt, if snooker worked out according to Euclid, players with a mathematical mind, a good eye and a good cue-action would pot or double everything on the board and no one ever need study the complications of the game at all. None of them is beyond solution, but together they make snooker a game of which no one will ever get to the end.

SOME TECHNICAL TERMS

Cue-ball
The cue-ball is the ball of the striker; all other balls are object balls.

To play from hand
To play from hand the striker must play the cue-ball from some position on or within the lines of the 'D'.

Ball in baulk
A ball is 'in baulk' when it rests on the baulk-line or between that line and the bottom cushion.

Ball off the table
A ball is forced off the table which comes to rest otherwise than on the bed of the table or in a pocket.

A stroke
A stroke is made by a player touching his ball, or striking his ball when it is in play, with the tip of his cue. No stroke is completed until all balls have come to rest and the player is adjudged to have left the table.

A break
A break is a series of consecutive scoring strokes made in any one turn.

A miss
A miss is a stroke where the cue-ball fails to touch any
other ball.

Spot occupied

A spot or position is said to be occupied if a ball cannot be placed thereon without touching or disturbing another ball.

GENERAL RULES

A fair stroke

All strokes must be made with the tip of the cue. The ball must be struck and not pushed. The ball must not be struck more than once in the same stroke either before or after contact with another ball. At the moment of striking, one of the player's feet must touch the floor.

A foul stroke

Is one made in contravention of any Rule of the Game being played. (See Rules, pp. 51–2.)

Ball on edge of pocket

If the ball which falls is part of the stroke, that stroke shall be void, the balls placed in their original position and the stroke replayed. If the ball is not an integral part of the stroke, the stroke shall stand and the ball which fell only shall be replaced. If it balances momentarily on the edge and falls in, it must not be replaced.

The jump shot

The jump shot is a foul in which the cue-ball is made to jump over any ball whether by accident or design. The penalty is the value of the ball *on* or value of the ball struck, or value of the ball pocketed, whichever is the higher.

The push stroke

A push stroke is a foul and is made when the tip of the cue remains in contact with the cue-ball when the cue-ball itself makes contact with the object-ball, or when the tip of the cue remains in contact with the cue-ball after the cue-ball has commenced its forward motion.

Penalty: as for the jump shot.

The referee

The Referee shall be the sole judge of fair or unfair play, and shall be responsible for the proper conduct of the game under the Rules, and shall of his own initiative intervene if he sees any contravention. He shall, on appeal by a player, and on appeal only, decide any question of fact connected with play. If he has failed to observe any incident, he may take the evidence of the spectators best placed for observation, to assist his decision. He shall decide all questions arising between the players on the interpretations of the rules. The Referee shall not give any advice or express opinion on points affecting play.

The Rules of Snooker

Authorised by the Billiards and Snooker Control Council

1
Definition
of Game

The game of *Snooker* (or Snooker's Pool) is played on an English Billiard Table, and may be played by two or more persons, either as sides, or independently. It is a game of winning hazards; cannons are ignored. The winner is the player or side making the highest score, or to whom the game, under Rule 14, is awarded.

The balls

2
Number
in set

The set of balls should be twenty-two in number, consisting of fifteen reds, one black, one pink, one blue, one brown, one green, one yellow and a white ball, which is called the cue-ball. In the game on the B. & S. C. C. 6 ft. Standard Table the set of balls shall be seventeen in number, consisting of ten reds, one black, one pink, one blue, one brown, one green, one yellow and a white ball, which is called the cue-ball.

Technical terms

3 a

The white ball is referred to as the *cue-ball*; the yellow, green, brown, blue, pink and black, as the *pool balls*, or *colours*, the red (or pyramid) balls as *reds*.

b
Ball forced
off Table

Any ball which is forced off the table becomes out of play, but, with the exception of a red ball, is immediately replaced upon its allotted spot.

c
Ball 'On'
To Play at
Balls

A player is said to be *on* a ball when such ball may be lawfully struck by the cue-ball under these Rules. He is *on* a pool ball nominated under Rules 5 and 10.

d
Player
Snookered

A player is said to be *snookered* with regard to any ball when a direct stroke in a straight line of the cue-ball to any point of such ball is obstructed by any ball which is not *on*. If a player is *in hand* after a foul, he cannot be *snookered* with regard to any ball that is *on*, if he can get a direct stroke in a straight line from some part of the 'D' (*i.e.*, a clear ball).

47

When the ball *on* is snookered by more than one ball, the effective snookering ball is the one nearest to the cue-ball.

e **Cue-ball Angled** The cue-ball is said to be *angled* when the corner of the cushion prevents a stroke being made, in a straight line, directly on any part of any ball that may be lawfully struck.

f **Nominated Ball** A *Nominated Ball* is the object-ball which the striker declares he undertakes to strike with the first impact of the cue-ball.

4 **Placing the Balls** Fifteen reds in the form of a triangle, the ball at the apex standing as near to the pink ball as possible, without touching it; the base being parallel with and nearest to the top cushion: BLACK on the BILLIARD SPOT; PINK on the PYRAMID SPOT; BLUE on the CENTRE SPOT; BROWN on the MIDDLE of the baulk-line; GREEN on the LEFT-HAND and YELLOW on the RIGHT-HAND corner of the 'D'.

5 **Mode of Play** Players must first determine by lot, or other convenient method, the order of their turn, which must remain unaltered throughout the game. The first player shall play from hand. The

First Stroke cue-ball shall strike a red as the initial stroke of each turn, until all the reds are off the table. The value of each red, lawfully pocketed by the same stroke, is scored. For the next stroke of the turn (if a score is made) the cue-ball shall strike a pool ball, the value of which (if lawfully pocketed) is scored. The game is continued by pocketing reds, and pool balls, alternately, in the same turn. If the striker fails to score, the player next in turn plays from where the cue-ball

Cue-Ball Pocketed came to rest. If the cue-ball is pocketed or forced off the table, the next player plays from hand. Once the cue-ball has come to rest on the table after a foul has been committed it must be played from where it has come to rest. Each *pool ball* pocketed or forced off the table must be

Re-spotting the Balls Last Red re-spotted before the next stroke, until finally pocketed under these Rules. If the player who lawfully pockets the last red, pocket any pool ball with his next stroke, this ball is re-spotted. Otherwise (reds being off the table) the pool

Pocketing Pool Balls balls must be struck by the cue-ball in the progressive order of their values and *if lawfully pocketed* are not re-spotted. When requested

48 **Nominating** by the referee a player must state which ball he

	is *on*. He is advised to do so for his own
Intentional	protection. An intentional miss shall not be
Miss	made. The player shall, to the best of his ability,
	endeavour to strike a ball that is *on*.
First Impact	The first impact of the cue-ball shall govern all
	strokes.
EXAMPLE	A player *on* blue makes the first impact with the

is *on*. He is advised to do so for his own protection. An intentional miss shall not be made. The player shall, to the best of his ability, endeavour to strike a ball that is *on*.

First Impact The first impact of the cue-ball shall govern all strokes.

EXAMPLE A player *on* blue makes the first impact with the cue-ball on the blue, the cue-ball then strikes the black or any other ball and goes into a pocket the player is penalised five points, the value of the blue, the ball on which the cue-ball made the first impact.

6

Ball Values The scoring values of the balls are: red —1, yellow—2, green—3, brown—4, blue—5, pink—6, black—7.

7

Re-spotting Pool Balls The striker must see that every ball required to be re-spotted is properly placed before he plays his stroke. *Reds* are never re-spotted. Any pool ball pocketed by a foul stroke is not deemed to have been lawfully pocketed, and shall be re-spotted. If the spot, named in Rule 4 for each pool ball, is occupied when such ball shall be placed thereon, the ball shall be placed on the spot first named in Rule 4, that is then unoccupied, i.e., if the spot allocated to the yellow is occupied by another ball, after the yellow has been pocketed, then the yellow ball is to be placed on the black spot, or, if that is occupied, then on the pink spot, and so on. If all the spots are occupied, any pool ball other than the black and pink shall be placed as near its own spot as possible between that spot and the *nearest part* of the top cushion without touching another ball. In the case of the black and pink balls being potted and all the spots are occupied, they shall be placed as near as possible to their own spots, up the table, on the centre line of the table, and without touching another ball. If the space between the black spot and the top cushion is occupied, the black ball shall be placed as near as possible to the black spot, on the centre line of the table, below its spot, and without touching another ball. Similarly if the space between the pink spot and the top cushion is occupied, the pink shall be placed as near as possible to the pink spot, on the centre line of the table, below its spot, and without touching another ball.

Balls struck simultaneously or pocketed on one stroke
NOTE

9 a
Cue-ball Touching

b

c

EXAMPLES
(1)

(2)

(3)

(4)

10
Snookering After a foul

Two balls (other than two reds or the ball 'on' and the ball nominated under Rule 10) must not be struck simultaneously nor pocketed by the same stroke.

Any number of red balls may be pocketed by one stroke made in accordance with these rules.

If the cue-ball is touching another ball which is *on*, the striker must play away from the touching ball without moving the latter, or he must be held to have pushed. The striker thus playing away from a ball *on* shall incur no penalty for a miss or for striking another ball, but he may lawfully pocket any other ball which is *on*. If he pockets a ball which is not *on*, he forfeits the penalty under Rule 12

If the cue-ball is touching another ball which is not *on*, the striker must play away from such ball as in (a). If the ball *on* is missed, or another ball hit, the penalty as laid down in Rule 12 must be forfeited.

In all cases where the cue-ball is touching the ball *on* or touching a colour after a red has been potted, the referee shall state 'TOUCHING BALL' without being asked. If the cue-ball is touching more than one ball 'on' he shall, on request, state which ball(s) the cue-ball is touching. He shall offer no other information.

The *ball on is red*, cue-ball is *touching red*, striker plays away from red without disturbing it, strikes and goes in off black. The penalty is four points, the value of the ball *on*.

The *ball on is yellow*, cue-ball is *touching yellow*, striker plays away from yellow without disturbing it and pockets black. The penalty is seven points, the value of the ball *pocketed*.

The *ball on is red*, cue-ball is *touching black*, striker plays away from black without disturbing it, misses all balls and cue-ball enters a pocket. The penalty is four points, the value of the ball *on*.

In the case of the striker, playing away from black, missing all reds and striking blue he is penalised five points.

After a foul stroke, if the striker be snookered (a) *with regard to all reds* he is then *on* any ball he may nominate, and for all purposes such nominated ball shall be regarded as a red, except that, if pocketed, it shall be spotted; (b) After a foul stroke, if the striker be snookered, (*reds being off the table*) *with regard to the pool ball on*, he is then *on* any ball he may nominate, and for all purposes such nominated ball shall be regarded as the ball *on*, except that should it be lawfully pocketed it shall be spotted, and the player shall continue his break on the ball he was *on*, but for being snookered. If, as a result of playing on the nominated ball, the ball *on* be pocketed, it shall be scored and the player continues his break.

Nominated Should both the nominated ball and the ball *on*
Ball and be pocketed by the same stroke, only the ball *on*
Ball 'on' shall be scored, and the player continues his
Pocketed break. The nominated ball only shall be re-spotted.

Snookered by the Should the striker leave the opponent snookered
Nominated ball by the nominated ball it is a foul stroke, except when only pink and black remain on the table.

Missing the ball Should the striker fail to hit the ball nominated
Nominated under this Rule it is a foul stroke.

11 If the cue-ball is angled it must be played from
Cue-ball where it lies; but if angled after a foul, it may be
Angled played from hand, at the striker's discretion.

12 A player who contravenes any Rule of this game:
Penalties (a) cannot score; (b) loses his turn; (c) forfeits such points as are exacted in these Rules— which are added to his opponent's score; (d) in addition, the striker has the option of playing from where the balls have come to rest, or requesting the opponent to play the stroke; (e) minimum penalty for any infringement is four points.

13 The player contravenes these rules by the
Foul Strokes following acts (among others):

a By making a losing hazard. Penalty, value of ball *on*, or value of ball struck, whichever is the higher.

b By causing the cue-ball to strike a ball he is not *on*. Penalty, value of the ball struck, or value of the ball *on*, whichever is the higher.

c By making a miss. Penalty, value of the ball *on*.

d By snookering his opponent with the nominated ball after a foul stroke, except when only pink and black remain. Penalty, value of the ball *on*.

e By striking simultaneously or pocketing with one stroke two balls, except two reds, or the ball *on* and the ball nominated. Penalty, highest value of the two struck, or pocketed.

f   By moving an object-ball in contravention of Rule 9. (Cue-ball Touching.) Penalty, value of the ball *on*, or value of the ball moved, whichever is the higher.

g   By forcing a ball off the table. Penalty, the value of the ball *on*, or value of the ball forced off the table, whichever is the higher.

h   By pocketing any ball not *on*. Penalty, value of the ball *pocketed*, or value of the ball *on*, whichever is the higher.

i   For playing with other than the cue-ball. Penalty seven points.

j   By playing at two reds in successive strokes. Penalty, seven points.

k   By using a dead ball to test whether a ball will pass another, or go on a spot, for any other purpose. Penalty, seven points.

l   By playing with both feet off the floor. Penalty, value of the ball *on*, or value of the ball struck, or value of the ball pocketed or value of the ball improperly spotted, whichever is the higher.

m   By playing before the balls have come to rest, or before they have been spotted or when wrongly spotted. Penalty, value of the ball *on*, or value of the ball struck, or value of the ball wrongly spotted, or value of the ball pocketed, whichever is the higher.

n   By striking or touching a ball whilst in play, otherwise than with the tip of the cue. Penalty, value of the *ball struck* or *touched*, or value of the ball *on*, whichever is the higher.

o   By playing improperly from hand. Penalty, value of the ball *on*, or value of the ball struck, or value of the ball pocketed, or value of the ball improperly spotted, whichever is the higher.

p   Push Stroke. Penalty, value of the ball *on*, or value of the ball struck, or value of the ball pocketed, whichever is the higher.

q   Jump Shot. Penalty, value of the ball *on*, or value of the ball struck, or value of the ball pocketed, whichever is the higher.

r   By playing out of turn. Penalty, value of the ball *on*, or value of the ball struck, or value of the ball pocketed, whichever is the higher.

s   Failing to nominate when awarded a free ball, penalty to be the value of the ball struck, or value of the ball pocketed, or if no ball is struck, the value of the ball *on*.

Official Decisions Only the referee is allowed to clean a ball on the table. He should do so at a player's request.

It is the striker's responsibility to see that the balls are correctly spotted before playing his stroke.

If the referee considers that a player is taking an abnormal amount of time over his stroke, with the intention of upsetting his opponent, the referee should warn him that he runs the risk of being disqualified if he pursues these tactics.

A player should not be penalised if, when using the rest, the rest head falls off and touches a ball.

Unless a foul stroke is awarded by the referee, or claimed by the non-striker, before the next stroke is made, it is condoned.

If the striker plays with the balls improperly spotted, he scores all points made until the foul is awarded by the referee, or claimed by the non-striker.

The referee should not give any indication that a player is about to make a foul stroke.

If the striker makes a miss, the referee can order him to re-play the stroke penalising him the requisite forfeit for each miss, but he scores all points in any subsequent stroke.

When snookered after a foul stroke, a player must nominate the ball he intends to play.

If at the opening stroke of a game the striker fails to hit a red, the next player plays from where the cue-ball has come to rest.

A Snooker A player must be able to strike both sides of the ball *on* free of obstruction from any ball or balls not *on*. It virtually means the diameter of a ball on either side of the ball *on*.

If a player is colour blind, the referee should tell him the colour of a ball if requested.

A referee must declare when a player has a free ball without appeal from a player.

Examples of Foul Strokes
(1) *Red is the ball on*, striker fouls *the black* with his cue or otherwise, the penalty is seven points, the value of the *ball fouled*.

(2) *Black is the ball on*, striker fouls *a red* with his cue or arm, the penalty is seven points, the value of the *ball on*.

(3) A player pots the *pink* and before it is

properly spotted he pots a *red* ball — what is the penalty?

Decision: six points for playing with the balls not properly spotted (value of the ball not properly spotted).

Wilful Evasion of Spirit of Rules If a game is awarded to a player under Rule 15 GENERAL RULES, the offender shall lose the game, and forfeit all points he may have scored, or the value of the balls on the table (reds = 8 each) whichever is higher.

14
End of Game and Tie

When only the black ball is left, the first score or forfeit ends the game, unless the scores are then equal, in which case the black is spotted, and the players draw lots for choice of playing at the black from hand. The next score or forfeit ends the game. In games (whether individuals, pairs or teams) where aggregate points decide the winner, it is only when the scores are equal *AS A RESULT OF THE LAST FRAME*, that the black is re-spotted. The next score or forfeit ends the game.

RULE CHANGE

As from 1 December 1973, players will not be required to nominate their colour when taking a free ball unless there is doubt over which ball the player is attempting.

Pot Black Postbag

During *Pot Black*'s sixteen-week run there is always a very heavy load of correspondence from viewers. Apart from those commenting, favourably or otherwise, about the programmes, many viewers use *Pot Black* as an Advice Bureau, and deluge us with questions, the answers to which often demand a certain amount of ingenuity, not to mention research. The questions vary a lot, but the most popular, even though we have given the answer on the air in an attempt to reduce the postbag, concerns the highest break a player can achieve in snooker. This particular query will in time become a classic at any snooker quiz. So what is the answer? A break of 155 is technically possible, which would come about if a foul stroke was committed at the break-off. This would give the opponent a free ball counting as a red (one point) and by taking the black he could add 8 points to the accepted maximum break of 147. As far as is known, no player has ever achieved a break of 155, and so for obvious reasons the maximum break is recognised by the world governing body as 147.

Now let us look at what I would describe as being typical *Pot Black* posers.

Q   Is it a foul stroke if, when commencing a game, the striker fails to strike a red?
A   It is 4 away and the opponent takes his turn from where the cue-ball has come to rest.

Q   Is it a foul shot if a player strikes a cushion before hitting the red at the opening stroke of the game?
A   No.

Q   In a match of more than one frame does the player who has potted the black in the previous game break off in the next frame?
A   Not necessarily so. The break should run alternately and be decided by the spin of a coin when an odd number of games are played

Q When addressing the cue-ball at the opening stroke of the game the player accidentally touches the ball with the tip of his cue. Can he replace the ball and play again or does he play the cue-ball from the position where it had come to rest?

A At the slightest touch of the ball the player must leave the table and allow his opponent to play from where the cue-ball has come to rest. There is also a penalty of 4 points

Q Is the player allowed to play the cue-ball against a cushion without making an attempt to hit the pack of reds at the opening stroke of the game?

A Definitely no. He must at all times make an attempt to strike the 'ball on'.

Q What is the penalty if a player plays his shot with both feet off the floor?

A The penalty is the value of the 'ball on'.

Q Is there any penalty when the striker's tie, coat, shirt sleeve, or any other part of his person touches a ball, even though it does not move it?

A Yes, the penalty is the value of the 'ball on', or the value of the ball touched if it is of higher value.

Q What is the penalty when the cue-ball is forced off the table?

A It is the value of the 'ball on' and the next player plays from the D.

Q What is the penalty when the cue-ball and object-ball are forced off the table?

A Again, the value of the 'ball on', and if it is a coloured ball it is re-spotted.

Q What is the position if a player pockets more than one red by the same stroke?

A One point is scored for each red pocketed.

Q Player on a red strikes it, then cannons on to the black, or another colour, and runs into a pocket. Is the penalty 4 or 7 points?

A The penalty is only 4 points.

Q Player on a red strikes it, then cannons on to the black, or any other colour, which falls into a pocket. What is the penalty?

A   In this case the penalty is a minimum of 4 points unless the colour potted is of higher value, when it is the value of the colour potted.

Q   After potting a red ball is the player allowed to roll the cue-ball behind a coloured ball leaving a deliberate snooker?

A   Yes, this move is a fair shot.

Q   After potting a red a player inadvertently pockets another red instead of a colour. What is the penalty?

A   It is 7 away. The highest valued ball on the table.

Q   Having potted a coloured ball the striker inadvertently pots another colour. How many points are forfeited?

A   Four points or the value of the second colour potted, if higher

Q   Striker misses the pack of red balls which is a foul stroke giving 4 away. His opponent is not actually snookered, but he cannot strike any particular red on either extreme edge. Can he claim a free ball?

A   You cannot claim a free ball if you are only prevented from striking both sides of a 'ball on' by the intervention of another 'ball on' or a cushion.

Q   My opponent having gone 'in off' a red leaves me in position that I cannot strike the 'ball on' full in the face *from any part* of the D. Can I claim to be snookered and have a free ball?

A   Definitely a free ball when you *cannot* strike the 'ball on' at any point from any part of the D.

Q   What is a free ball?

A   A player snookered after a foul shot by his opponent may nominate to play any coloured ball (a 'free ball'). If reds are still on the table, the nominated ball, if potted, counts one point (as a red). If the nominated (free) ball is potted and there are no reds left on the table, the score is the value of the lowest colour left on the table.

Q   What is a plant?

A   A position where two (or more) object-balls are played on to each other so that the second (or last) object-ball is potted.

Pot (Black) Pourri

DID YOU KNOW THAT ...

Alex 'Hurricane' Higgins made a break of 122 against Patsy Fagan during the Irish Professional Championship at the Ulster Hall, Belfast, in 2 minutes 45 seconds?

Jimmy White, from Tooting, became the youngest-ever English Amateur Snooker champion, winning just one month before his seventeenth birthday?

The Guild of Television Cameramen awarded a Certificate of Merit to the BBC camera team at Pebble Mill, Birmingham, for outstanding camera work throughout the *Pot Black* series?

Joe Davis's own snooker table was sold at Sotheby's for £10,000 and subsequently won in a competition by the Post Office Supplies Club, Swindon?

The *Pot Black* signature-tune 'Black and White Rag' played by Winifred Atwell is featured in the BBC LP 'Sporting Themes'?

Willie Thorne, playing with both legs in plaster after an accident, made his fourteenth maximum break at his own club in Leicester?

Nearly ten million viewers watched the 1982 *Pot Black* final between Steve Davis and Eddie Charlton?

Mike Watterson, the promoter of the 1982 Embassy World Championships, was beaten by Jim Meadowcroft in that event?

There are 'Pot Black' Snooker centres in London, Reading and Plymouth?

Pot Black commentator, Ted Lowe, is the new President of the Billiards and Snooker Control Council?

Steve Davis and Tony Meo were featured on Bangkok TV playing Thailand's leading players in August 1982?

DID YOU KNOW THAT . . .

John Spencer is the owner of the club 'Spencer's' in Bolton, complete with snooker room, restaurant and bar?

Joyce Gardner, the Women's Professional Billiards Champion from 1930 to 1938, died in September 1981?

Benny Green, the journalist and broadcaster, voted *Pot Black* and BBC cricket coverage as the best sports programmes of 1978? (*Punch*, Dec. 78)

A plaque to commemorate Joe Davis's birthplace, 80 Welbeck Street, Whitwell, Derbyshire, was unveiled by his widow, June, and his brother, Fred, on 16 December 1978?

Perrie Mans' father, Peter Mans, played in the quarter-finals of the 1950 World Snooker Championship?

Billiards and Snooker are included in the Interests section of the Duke of Edinburgh Award Scheme?

Willie Smith, the 1920 World Professional Billiards Champion, died at his home in Leeds in June 1982 at the age of 96?

Jack Karnehm, the TV commentator and 1980 UK Professional Billiards Champion, is the proprietor of the 'Berkshire' Snooker Club in Windsor?

Pot Black compère, Alan Weeks, is a director of the British Sports Aid Foundation?

Joe O'Boye, the 1980 English Amateur Champion, is managed by the former England goalkeeper, Gordon Banks?

John Parrott (Liverpool), the 1982 *Junior Pot Black* Champion, also won the Pontin's 'Open' (against Ray Reardon) and the Silver Cue competition at La Reserve, Sutton Coldfield, the same year?

Joe Davis's break of 100, telerecorded in 1962 for *Grandstand* and subsequently 'lost', was rediscovered in 1982 and shown during the World Championship transmissions from Sheffield?

Pot Black: Personalities and tips from the top

Eddie Charlton

Born in Merewether, New South Wales, on 31 October 1929, Eddie lived most of his life in Swansea, a coal-mining and fishing area ninety miles north of Sydney, where his grandfather had a small three-table billiard saloon. Eddie started playing about the age of nine, and by his eleventh birthday he could beat anybody in town.

In 1940 Walter Lindrum heard of Eddie's prowess and wrote to his grandfather asking him to bring Eddie to Sydney to play an exhibition. The invitation was accepted and Eddie played Walter one afternoon before a crowd of approximately 600 people, and that really was the commencement of the billiard and snooker career of Eddie Charlton. Eddie continued his education at his local secondary school in Swansea and then became a trainee apprentice fitter in the coal-mining industry.

Eddie completed twenty-two years in the coal mines in the New South Wales coalfield, and for all that time played soccer, the last twelve years First Division. For a similar period he joined in the Surf Life Saving Movement which meant that he virtually trained hard all winter and summer for those twenty-two years. 'I was so fit in those days it frightens me to think back on it compared with today.'

One of the highlights in his surfing career was to be a member of the Swansea Belmont Senior Surf Boat crew who won the Australian title in 1950 at Coolangatta, Queensland. During this time he also played 'A' grade tennis, 'A' reserve grade cricket, golf, squash, and through his amateur boxing career managed to win three amateur boxing titles and had the pleasure of boxing in four exhibitions with the late Dave Sands. Eddie was also a member of an athletic club and when the Olympic Games were held in Melbourne in 1956 the Olympic flame, having been flown from Greece to Darwin, was carried by

runners over 3000 miles to Melbourne. Each runner carried the torch one mile. Eddie's brother Jim carried it the mile into Swansea and Eddie the mile out of Swansea. He still feels that this was one of the most exciting activities of his sporting career.

As an amateur he won three New South Wales State snooker titles and one New South Wales billiards title. He turned professional in 1960 and has held the Australian professional snooker title each year but one.

Among the titles he has held are: New South Wales Open Snooker Championship; New South Wales Professional Snooker Championship; Australian Professional Snooker Championship; Australian Match Play Snooker Championship; Australian Open Snooker Championship; British Commonwealth Open Snooker Championship; *Pot Black* Champion 1972, 1973 and 1980.

In the first of his attempts at the World Professional Snooker title he was beaten by John Pulman in the 1968 Final. In 1970 he was beaten in the semi-final, 1972 again beaten in a semi-final, 1973 beaten in the Final by Ray Reardon. Surprisingly, in 1974 he failed to reach the quarter-finals, but with the 1975 World Championships being played virtually on his doorstep, the Australian came within one frame of taking the title from Ray Reardon. In 1976 Eddie lost to Alex Higgins in the semi-finals, and later unsuccessfully challenged Rex Williams for the World Billiards title. At Sheffield in the 1977 World Championships he met the Canadian Champion, Cliff Thorburn, in the quarter-finals and lost by just one frame, 13–12. Twelve months later the same two players met again in the quarter-finals and on this occasion the result and the score were reversed when Eddie beat Cliff by the odd frame. However, his hope of reaching the Final disappeared when Ray Reardon defeated him by 18 frames to 14 in the semi-finals.

Since entering the World Championship in 1968, Eddie has often been involved in the closing stages. In 1979 he survived until the semi-finals, beating Doug Mountjoy and Fred Davis, but losing then to Terry Griffiths, who was to become the new World Champion, by only 19 frames to 17. Consolation for Eddie followed when he beat John Virgo in the 13-frame 'Play Off' for third place. In the 1980 World Championship, after beating John Virgo again in the second round, he lost in the quarter-finals by 13–7 to the young Canadian Kirk Stevens.

Eddie has sacrificed Christmas in the Australian sunshine since 1972 to play in *Pot Black* (the programme is recorded just after Christmas). His efforts have been rewarded as he won the *Pot Black* Trophy for the third time in 1980, and no one has yet bettered his highest break in the series of 110, which he achieved in 1973.

At home in Sydney, Eddie combines playing with the management of a successful billiards company and the organisation of tournaments. He is the author of two books on snooker and, as one of the most popular players in *Pot Black*, his appearances have contributed to the success of the television series both in Australia and New Zealand. His contributions to the success of *Pot Black* were gratefully recognised in 1981 when he received the 'Personality Award' – a silver replica of the *Pot Black* Trophy. Later in the year he failed to win his second-round game against Doug Mountjoy in the World Championship but made a welcome return visit to the Pebble Mill studios shortly afterwards. There Eddie presented the new *Junior Pot Black* Trophy to the winner, 18-year-old Dean Reynolds from Grimsby.

The Australian trio of Charlton (captain), Ian Anderson and Paddy Morgan, lost to England 4–3 (after a tie-break frame) and to Northern Ireland by 4–1 in the 1981 State

Express World Team Classic at the Hexagon Theatre, Reading. Eddie returned to Pebble Mill, Birmingham, in December 1981 to compete in his eleventh consecutive *Pot Black*. It was also to be his fourth appearance in the Final, but he was runner-up on this occasion to the 1981 World Champion Steve Davis. Eddie won the highest break prize for the third time, with a score of 98. In the 1982 Benson and Hedges Masters the Australian was beaten 5–1 by Alex Higgins in the quarter-finals, and his next major tournament was the World Championship. He has always tried extremely hard to win this title and once again reached the semi-finals. Ray Reardon – the man who had beaten Eddie in the 1973 and 1975 finals – was, yet again, to bring Eddie's chances to an end for another year, by 16 frames to 11. Eddie enters the coming season fifth in the world rankings list.

Fred Davis

One of the most famous names of the Snooker world, Fred Davis was born at Whittingham Moor, near Chesterfield, the younger brother of the legendary Joe Davis by some twelve years. He became Boys Billiards Champion at 15 and, following his brother's example, gradually turned to the more popular game of snooker.

In 1940 Fred met brother Joe for the World title and lost by only one frame, 36 to 37. His first World Championship title was gained in 1948 against the late Walter Donaldson. Since then Fred has won the World Championship on nine occasions, including the officially unrecognised game against George Chenier of Canada in 1958. One of his proudest achievements was his defeat of his brother in the *Empire News* tournament in 1948. He was also the holder of the UK Professional Billiards title, which he won by beating Kingsley Kennerley in 1951.

He played in all the *Pot Black* series from 1969 to 1973, and won the Highest Break prize in 1970 and 1971. Ill-health prevented Fred from appearing in the 1974 *Pot Black* competition and he was ordered by his doctor to take a complete rest.

He returned to compete in the World Championships at Belle Vue Manchester in April 1974. Although lacking in match practice, Fred, now 62, played superbly. His victory over the Canadian Champion, Bill Werbeniuk, took him into the quarter-finals to face the formidable Alex Higgins. Davis won by 15 frames to 14 but the following day this struggle had obviously affected Fred's stamina and he failed against Reardon in the semi-finals.

Fred was once again a member of the 1975 *Pot Black* 'squad', winning the Highest Break prize with a score of 87. His cheque was presented to him after the final frame by his brother Joe.

Fred started the 1976 *Pot Black* series off well by beating Willie Thorne, some forty years his junior, by 88 points to 28. However, he lost against Rex Williams and Dennis Taylor in later rounds. In the World Championships at Manchester he battled bravely against Eddie Charlton in the quarter-finals to lose by just two frames.

He failed to reach the quarter-finals of the 1977 World Championship at Sheffield, being beaten in the first round by his old rival John Pulman. However, later that year Fred was to have the consolation of being awarded the OBE for services to snooker. This makes a unique snooker 'double' as his brother Joe had also been awarded the OBE some years earlier.

Back in the Championship for the 1978 World title Fred was in excellent form and, wearing contact lenses instead of his famous 'swivel-lens' spectacles, he defeated two much younger players, Dennis Taylor and the UK Professional Champion Patsy Fagan. This took him into the semi-finals but, in spite of a tremendous display of his old skills, his opponent from South Africa, Perrie Mans, finally won the game by 18 frames to 16.

Fred was, once again, among the eight players in *Pot Black* 1979, where he played – and lost to – the young Steve Davis and Perrie Mans. His only victory, over the defending Champion, Doug Mountjoy, was not enough to see him through to the semi-finals. He was defeated by Eddie Charlton in the 1979 World Championship quarter-finals after winning his first-round match against the Canadian Kirk Stevens.

Another disappointment for Fred in early 1979 came when he unsuccessfully defended his 28-year-old title of UK Professional Billiards Champion. He lost his semi-final game to another name of the past, John Barrie, by 1548 points to 1031. However, Fred did reach the Final of
the Castle Open competition at the Castle Club, South-

ampton, beating Willie Thorne and Cliff Thorburn. Although, at the age of 65, he lost to Alex Higgins in the Final, he shared the enthusiastic applause given to both players at the end of the game.

Throughout the remainder of 1979 and on into 1980, Fred continued to compete at both billiards and snooker. He played for England, with John Spencer and Graham Miles, in the State Express World Cup, making breaks of 55 and 63. His other engagements included the Coral UK at Preston, the Padmore/Super Crystalate International, the Benson and Hedges Masters, the British Gold Cup, the Pontin's Festival and, of course, the World Championship at Sheffield. At the age of 66 he realised a lifelong ambition when, in May 1980, he won the Yorkshire Bank-sponsored World Professional Billiards Championship in a challenge match against the holder, Rex Williams. Played over four days at the Northern Snooker Centre in Leeds, the final scores were: Davis 5978 points, Williams 4452. Fred now joins his late brother Joe as the only players to have won both the World Billiards and World Snooker Championships.

In November 1980, Fred successfully defended his World Billiards Champion title at the Brownsover Hall Hotel in Rugby. Among his opponents were Rex Williams, Jack Karnehm, Kingsley Kennerley and Steve Davis. The beaten finalist, however, was Mark Wildman of Peterborough who had been playing professionally for only twelve months. The UK Professional Billiards Championship, at the Winter Gardens, Margate, in February 1981 resulted in a semi-final defeat for Fred by his old rival, Rex Williams.

After a disappointing performance in the 1981 World Championship, Fred threatened to retire altogether from championship play. However, and not too surprisingly, he changed his mind and, after losing to Rex Williams in the semi-finals of the World Billiards Championship, Fred was once again at Sheffield for the World Snooker Championship. Seeded 12, the oldest player lost to the youngest player, Dean Reynolds, the 1981 *Junior Pot Black* Champion, by 10 frames to 7 in the first round.

ESSENTIALS OF GOOD POTTING
by Fred Davis

It seems to me that some people have a good, straight steady cue action from the first moment they start to play. Within a few games they are banging down all the so-called easy ones without any trouble, and they get ahead with the rest of the game much quicker than others because they do not have to worry overmuch about whether the ball is going down or not. Others have potting troubles all their lives – even men who are good at the other departments of the game, players whose strength is good, who have an uncanny knowledge of the angles and who can lay a deadly snooker. It is almost pitiful to see them make a lovely positional shot and then fail to knock the colour in.

One of the reasons is a badly made bridge; another is a habit of moving some part of the body on the stroke. But there are players who conform in these respects and still cannot rely on their potting. They tell you that one day it seems easy, and the next even the simple ones are difficult. These players suffer from cue wobble. I should think the percentage is very high indeed, and the odd thing is that players who have been at the game for twenty years and play reasonably well on a club standard still suffer from it.

This is the complaint which I think you may never have or you may always have – unless you know how it is caused. It depends at the outset of your playing career on how you pick up and hold your cue. This, in turn, depends on the length of your cue, and its balance. Much of the trouble of side-to-side wobble is caused by having the cue-hold too far back. Ideally, the book tells us, the forearm, at rest, should drop perpendicularly from the elbow and the grip should be about one inch from the end of the butt. But it is ridiculous to lay down such rules. Cues in any club rack vary in length up to nine inches, and in weight as much as three ounces. Arm-lengths vary.

I believe in a short, sturdy cue, not because I am a short man but because I believe a short cue is better for snooker than a long one. Short back action means greater accuracy in the drive. I also believe in the cue-hold being slightly *in front* of the vertical, but I see many, many players whose grip is *behind* the vertical. When I point it out, they are surprised; they didn't know. I like to get as close to the shot as possible, because I find that the closer I get the more control I have over what I am doing. The long sawing movements with long cues, with flowing finishes, are not for this game. Snooker requires compactness.

I believe in a short back swing and a good follow-through, but even the follow-through must be strictly controlled, and the cue held rigidly on the line. A good follow-through doesn't mean a flowing, meandering action. I like to be well forward over the left knee to get into the shot, but this may not suit you – it depends on your height.

Another important point is to keep the cue running close to the body – that is, brushing against the waistcoat without being buried in it. All these factors make for compactness – elbow well up, hand slightly in advance of elbow, good solid grip on the cue, hand wrapped well round the cue, and no pencil grip: these build up to a short, level, reasonably wobble-proof cue movement. If you have any wobble at all you must rid yourself of it, and at once you will know the joys of really good potting.

Maybe I should mention one further point. Many have cue wobble because they stand facing the shot too squarely. Stand at an angle of 45 degrees. The turning of the trunk to face the line of the shot causes some necessary tightness and tension, which all helps to fix the stance firmly.

FRED DAVIS ON SNOOKER

Middle-aged snooker players are the Micawbers of the sporting world. They are always hoping that something will happen to their style of play which will make them a black or two better. Like golfers they never give up hope, and why should they?

I have, in fact, helped a number of men aged over fifty to play better, and there are some who will say they are playing better now than they did twenty years ago. This is because I was able to point out faults in their stance or action which they had never been aware of. Quite small alterations to stance, for instance, will immediately make a player feel more comfortable and enable him to keep his cue on the line.

It has yet to be proved that age really matters at all in snooker, beyond the pure fatigue of standing up for a dozen stiff frames a day in championship stuff. I know that some whose snooker is not what it was can be heard to plead that their eyesight is not so good. To me, that is nonsense. I couldn't see them so well in my early twenties, but I had the adjustment made to my spectacle frames and have worn glasses ever since. Plenty of top-class players wear glasses, and if youth is scoring well in the amateur championships, that is rather because the great players who are over fifty are mostly billiards players who have never concentrated on snooker to the same degree as the youngsters.

Still, to the hard-working office type, whose brain is active five days a week, and whose digestion perhaps is not what it was, some falling off is likely. What is to be done? First, I suggest, is to recognise that your eyesight is not to blame – or if it is, to do something about it. Second, you may find that the main trouble is deterioration of your power of coordination. In short, the timing is no longer so sweet. You tend to hurry to get the actual shot over, or you come up on the stroke. The faults which you always made are now worse, too. The trivial things, such as too tight a grip, or a sloppy bridge, or that all-too-flowing swing, are exaggerated. You worry about your failures.

Well, I don't get any younger either. So I can prescribe with first-hand knowledge of the disease of gradual ageing. My prescription is twofold. Chiefly, you must learn to play within your powers. Don't play when you are tired. Don't play too many frames without a rest. And when you rest, even while your opponent is in a break, relax! Don't play as if life itself depended on winning; for that creates tension, which is fatal to timing.

Try to discover for yourself a more leisurely technique. By this I mean that, without being careless, you should move casually to your stroke, avoid the shots you are quite sure you won't bring off, play for snookers when you know that for you that is better than the bravado type of attempt at potting, and generally use your head like the cunning old fox.

The second piece of advice is to get a good player to play a frame with you and tell you afterwards, quite frankly, why you are missing them. Often you'll be astonished at the advice he will give you. He will see things, and may tell you things he has known about your play for years. It's a curious thing that, although in golf anyone will offer you advice gratis and unasked, in snooker no one ever tells you unless you ask. Best of all, of course, is to have a couple of sessions with a professional. Any ordinary player, and I don't care how bad or how old he is, will benefit from a lesson from a pro, and do so practically at once.

There is also this matter of getting the chin down to the cue. Perhaps, owing to your maturing build, you now find this very difficult. If so, don't try. That great little Canadian, George Chenier, who was here some years ago, played with a semi-upright stance, almost like the style of old John Roberts, yet he made a break which was then the world's record, of 144. True he afterwards adopted the English style, but I doubt if he played better as a result. He proved that it isn't necessary to get the chin down to the level of the cue to play brilliant snooker. So why should you force yourself into a position which is a strain?

If you are in your fifties, you have plenty of good snooker in you yet, if you take it easy.

Steve Davis

In 1957, the year that Steve was born in Plumstead, London, the World Snooker Championship Trophy was still in the possession of the famous Davis brothers, Joe and Fred. As Steve Davis (no relation) said in 1980,

'When I was a kid, I dreamed of playing in the World Championship – it's probably every youngster's ambition.' Just twelve months later Steve not only realised that ambition for the second time, but had his own name inscribed upon that coveted cup as the 1981 World Champion.

Steve began playing snooker at the age of fifteen at a holiday camp. Coached mainly by his father, Steve won the All England Junior Billiards Championship in 1976, reaching the semi-finals of the corresponding snooker competition. In August 1977 he made the elusive break of 147, won the Lucania Pro-Am and National Championship and, for good measure, the London and Home Counties Silver Jubilee Tournament. He was then selected to play for the English International team in April 1978 and went on to win the Pontin's Open Championship, defeating Ray Reardon and Dennis Taylor.

Steve's next victory was in the CIU Snooker Tournament, and in one of his last matches as an amateur he retained his Lucania Pro-Am title with a comfortable win over Patsy Fagan. Playing for the first time in the Canadian Open Tournament, Steve defeated Willie Thorne 9–3 but lost to Alex Higgins in the quarter-finals. His application for professional status was accepted on 17 September 1978.

In December of that year Steve made his television début in *Pot Black*. His first opponent, fittingly enough, was Fred Davis – over forty years older in both age and experience. Showing no signs of being overawed by his illustrious adversary, Steve scored a convincing victory by 83 points to 23. The tables (or table) were turned against him in his next game when Doug Mountjoy won by 97 points to 26, and Steve's chances of staying in the competition faded when he lost to Perrie Mans 60–45.

1979 was also the first year that Steve qualified to enter the World Championship. He survived to the First Round by beating Ian Anderson (Australia) and Patsy Fagan (Ireland). Steve played well against the eventual finalist, Dennis Taylor, losing the 25-frame match by only 13–11. His next big engagement was the Pontin's Snooker Festival and, unlike 1978 when he received 30 points start from the established players, this time he; too, had to give 30 points start to his amateur opponents. There were 1034 entries and at the end of the mammoth tournament

the winner was – Steve Davis, who beat the up-and-coming English Amateur Champion Jimmy White in the Final.

Steve later toured throughout Great Britain in a challenge series against Fred Davis, playing at some twelve clubs and travelling several thousand miles. The last game was held at Steve's home club at Romford where he was the winner by 9–3. It was here, too, that Steve played Alex Higgins in a marathon best of 65 frames challenge match and beat the Irish Champion 33–23. Steve met Jimmy White again in the Canadian 'Open' in the autumn of 1979, scoring a convincing 9–3 victory in the seventh round, but in his next game – the quarter-finals – the opposition came from the Canadian Champion, Cliff Thorburn. Despite breaks of 92, 100 and 120, the Londoner lost by 9 frames to 6.

One of Steve's best performances in his young career was achieved during the 1980 World Championship. After having beaten Patsy Fagan in the first round, he knocked out Terry Griffiths, the reigning Champion, in the second round by 13 frames to 10! It looked as if his manager's prophecy was about to come true, but his opponent in the quarter-finals was Alex Higgins. Although losing by 13 frames to 9 it was during this match that Steve cleared the table with a break of 136, sharing the £1000 prize for the highest break in the tournament with the Canadian Kirk Stevens. At the Pontin's Festival at Prestatyn, shortly after the World Championship, Steve again beat Terry Griffiths but he played disappointingly against John Virgo in the semi-finals, losing by 5 frames to 3. Revenge, however, came swiftly. Just a few days later, and at another holiday camp, Warner's on Hayling Island, Steve won the £2000 first prize in the GAME 'Open' Tournament, beating Virgo by 4 frames to nil in the semi-finals on the way.

Steve's progress was now in the ascendant and in November 1980 he won the Coral United Kingdom Championship with a 16 frames to 6 victory over Alex Higgins. Four days later he took the Wilson's Classic against Dennis Taylor. One of his less successful competitions was in *Pot Black* 81, where he failed to reach the semi-finals. However, Steve hit the sporting headlines again when he won the first prize of £10,000 in the Yamaha Organs Trophy at Derby in March 1981, beating David Taylor 9–6 in the Final, and another £4000 in the John Courage English Professional Championship.

As the No. 13 seed, Steve then entered the World Championship at Sheffield for the second time. His success is now part of snooker history, but a reminder of the opponents he defeated – Jimmy White, Alex Higgins, Terry Griffiths, Cliff Thorburn and Doug Mountjoy – serves to illustrate just what a hard-fought and well-deserved victory he achieved.

The next twelve months were to be, perhaps, the most eventful in any snooker player's career in the game's history. Steve rapidly earned the reputation of being unbeatable – which he was – at least in the major tournaments for several months. His list of lucrative victories included the Jameson International, beating Dennis Taylor 9–0 in the Final, the State Express World Team Classic (as England's captain), the Coral UK, beating Terry Griffiths by 16 frames to 3, the Benson and Hedges Masters, again beating Terry Griffiths, the Yamaha Organs Trophy, the Tolly Cobbold Classic and, for good measure, the 1982 *Pot Black* Championship! True, Steve finished as runner-up in the Lada Classic to Griffiths, 9–8, but achieved the first televised 147 break, against John Spencer in the quarter-finals. He also lost to

Griffiths, 5–9, in the Benson and Hedges Irish Masters, and to Jimmy White, 9–11, in the Northern Ireland Classic.

Possibly no result since he won the 1981 World Championship was as sensational as Steve's defeat, by 10 frames to 1, by the 150-1 outsider, Tony Knowles, in the first round of the 1982 event. Davis was unable to explain this débâcle, but later admitted that Knowles had played well and 'he never made any mistakes to let me in'. Steve is ranked in fourth position for the 1983 season.

Ray Edmonds

A successful amateur for nearly two decades, Ray's name first appeared in the record books as the runner-up in the 1961 England Amateur Championship. He comes from Lincolnshire and was for many years his county's Snooker and Billiards Champion. He is now the manager of a painting and decorating company in Grimsby. Ray was beaten in the Northern Section final of the 1963 England Amateur Championship by Gary Owen and continued to be unsuccessful in this event until he won it in 1969 by 11 frames to 9 against Jonathan Barron. He was to be twice runner-up again in 1972 and 1973. At Cardiff in 1972, Ray defeated Jonathan Barron once more in the semi-finals of the World Amateur Championship, going on to

win in the final against the South African player, Mannie Francisco, by 11 frames to 10. Two years later in Dublin he retained his World Amateur title against Geoff Thomas (Wales) but, going for the hat-trick in Johannesburg in 1976, he lost in the quarter-finals.

Ray has been a professional since 1978 and his results in the World Championships to date are: 1979, lost to Roy Andrewartha, 9–8; 1980, lost to Dennis Taylor in the first round, 10–3; 1981, lost to John Spencer in the first round, 10–9. He was a semi-finalist in the 1981 John Courage English Professional Championship, losing to Steve Davis, 9–0. Ray's accomplished billiards playing, however, brought him two major victories in 1981 – the Guinness 'Open' on the Isle of Wight and the Midas 'Masters' at Margate.

In the 1982 Yamaha International Masters Ray reached the Group A semi-finals, winning against Dennis Taylor but losing to Steve Davis and John Virgo. He made another attempt at the World Billiards title in March at La Reserve, Sutton Coldfield, but again lost in the semi-finals, to Mark Wildman of Peterborough. Then his qualifying match for the 1982 World Snooker Championship (also at La Reserve) resulted in a 9–6 defeat by the 1981 *Junior Pot Black* Champion Dean Reynolds.

Patsy Fagan

A Dubliner by birth but now a Londoner by adoption, Patsy Fagan is one of snooker's up-and-coming younger professionals. As an amateur he reached the final of the English Championship against Ray Edmonds in 1974, losing by 11 frames to 7. He represented Ireland in the 1975–6 Home Internationals, winning two of his three matches including one against Willie Thorne. He was again the losing finalist for the Southern Championship in 1976 but scored a record break of 115 during the competition.

Fagan turned professional in 1976 and went on to defeat Jim Meadowcroft in the qualifying rounds of the 1977 World Championship before losing to Ray Reardon by 13 frames to 7 in the next round. The Irishman's reputation was really established in 1978 with victories over John Virgo and Doug Mountjoy to win the title of UK

Professional Champion in the contest sponsored by Super Crystalate. This was followed by another success in the Dry Blackthorne Cup at Wembley, when Fagan beat John Spencer and then Alex Higgins in the final.

In the 1978 World Championship Patsy defeated Higgins yet again to reach the quarter-finals. He took the last frame from Alex in a dramatic finish after both players had won 12 frames each. Unfortunately for Fagan, he met veteran Fred Davis in his old form in the next session and was forced to exit from the Championship gracefully with the score at Davis 13, Fagan 10.

Subsequent tournaments have not proved too encouraging for the Irish player's record book and he is still trying to recapture his earlier winning form. In the *Daily Mirror*'s 'Champion of Champions' he was beaten 6–1 by Ray Reardon in the semi-finals, and John Spencer also beat him during the first round of the Holsten Lager

International. Patsy's 1978 UK Professional title was defended unsuccessfully at the Guildhall, Preston, when he lost to David Taylor, 9–7, in the first round. He fared no better in the 1979 World Championship, with a 9–3 defeat in a preliminary round by the young Londoner, Steve Davis. He was a member of the 'Rest Of The World' team in the State Express World Challenge Cup, but neither he nor his two companions, Perrie Mans and Jimmy van Rensburg of South Africa, could make much impression on their opponents from England and Northern Ireland. Patsy did put up a better performance in the Coral UK Championship, beating Pat Hallet of Grimsby and Graham Miles before succumbing to Dennis Taylor in the quarter-finals. In the 1980 World Championship it was a case of history repeating itself when his chance of surviving the first round was destroyed once again by Steve Davis, who won by 10 frames to 6.

Patsy played again for Ireland in the 1980 State Express World Cup. Despite some individual victories, his team lost to Wales in the semi-finals. In the second round of the Coral UK Championship, Fagan, the 1977 winner, produced some of his best form to lose by one frame, 9–8, to Terry Griffiths. But the 1981 World Championship was, once again, unlucky when he failed to win his qualifying-round match, 9–7, against John Dunning.

The following twelve months again proved to be somewhat disappointing. Patsy lost to Alex Higgins, 5–3, in the second round of the Jameson International at Stockport, and in the Coral UK he exited in the first round against Mike Hallett of Grimsby. His form improved in the 1982 World Championship, albeit briefly, by beating David Taylor, 10–9, in the first round before he suffered another second-round defeat, 13–7, against the Canadian Kirk Stevens. In the 1982 Irish Professional Championship Patsy lost his second-round match against Tommy Murphy, 6–2.

Silvino Francisco

The dark-featured and skilful South African player made his UK and television début in the 1982 World Championship, where he created one of the first-round surprise results in defeating the No. 5 seed, Dennis Taylor. He then

beat *Junior Pot Black* Champion Dean Reynolds, to reach the quarter-finals but found that he was unable to overcome the former World Champion Ray Reardon, losing by 13 frames to 8.

Silvino was born in Cape Town in May 1946 of Portuguese descent. He was the South Africa Snooker Champion in 1968 and Billiards Champion in 1972. He won both titles on further occasions, emulating the achievements of his older and better-known brother, Manuel. For the remainder of the 1982 season Silvino remained in England for club and summer engagements. This will allow him to become 'acclimatised' to our own snooker-playing conditions and to continue his practice for a second tilt at the next World Championship as the seventeenth seed.

Terry Griffiths

Until the BBC Television and Press coverage of the 1979 World Championship from Sheffield, relatively few snooker enthusiasts were familiar with the name of Terry

Griffiths. He was born and still lives in Llanelli where he had a variety of jobs, including that of postman. Terry, born in 1947, started playing snooker around the age of fifteen in his local billiard halls. 'I started when I was young, but I never had any coaching. I watched and listened to other players.'

A natural ability at the game turned into a talent that entitled him to enter the Welsh Amateur Championships. He was the losing finalist in 1972 and was subsequently selected to represent Wales in Home International Matches. Terry won most of his games in these events between 1973 and 1976. Meanwhile, in 1975, he did, at last, win the Welsh Amateur Championship. In November 1976 he reached the quarter-finals of the World Amateur Championship in Johannesburg but lost to the South African player, van Rensburg, 5–3. Terry's next success was in the spring of 1977, winning the English Amateur Championship and overwhelming Sid Hood of Grimsby 13–3. In the spring of 1978 he won the title for the second time, against Joe Johnson of Bradford, 13–5. Shortly afterwards his application to turn professional was accepted.

Terry provided the snooker sensation of 1979 when he won the World Snooker Championship at his first attempt. Later in the year two narrow defeats prevented him from adding two more important titles to his crown: in the final of the Canadian 'Open', at Toronto, he lost by 17–16 to Cliff Thorburn; and again by 14–13 to John Virgo in the final of the Coral UK Championship at Preston. He was invited to compete in *Pot Black* 80 but did not reach the semi-finals, losing two games out of three. His major success in becoming World Champion, however, was recognised in January 1980 when Terry was the 'victim' of *This is Your Life*.

A few weeks later Terry was back in form when he beat Cliff Thorburn, John Spencer and Alex Higgins to win the Benson and Hedges Masters at the Wembley Conference Centre. His bid to become World Champion for the second year running, however, was foiled by the young London professional, Steve Davis, when they met in the second round at Sheffield's Crucible Theatre. Losing by 13 frames to 10 the Welshman would have to wait twelve months to have another chance of retrieving his title. Nevertheless, Terry swallowed his disappointment and

spent the rest of the competition adding his comments on the play from the vantage point of a seat in the BBC TV commentary box.

Terry enjoyed mixed fortunes during the following twelve months. In September he lost to Cliff Thorburn, 17–10, in the final of the Canadian Open. He was one of the winning Welsh team for the State Express World Cup, played at the New London Theatre. A heavy defeat in the Coral UK Championship semi-finals, 9–0, by Steve Davis followed in November, and he lost to Alex Higgins in the Benson and Hedges Masters final, 9–6, in January and to Ray Reardon, also 9–6, in the semi-finals of the Woodpecker Welsh Professional Championship in February. But that month Terry retained his title in the Benson and

Hedges Irish Masters tournament with a prize of £5000 after defeating Ray Reardon, 9–7. The 1981 World Championship, unhappily for the 1979 Champion, brought him against Steve Davis for the second year running and once again Terry lost to the Londoner, by 13 frames to 9 in the quarter-finals. In the Pontin's Professional tournament, shortly after, Terry beat Steve 5–2 in the first round, going on to win the competition, 9–8, against Willie Thorne.

September 1982 saw Terry beaten by Alex Higgins, 5–2, in the quarter-finals of the Jameson International, and winning a minor event against Fred Davis at the Sheffield Snooker Centre. In October the Welsh team of Griffiths, Mountjoy and Reardon were the beaten finalists in the State Express World Team Classic. Terry's next important tournament was the Coral UK at the Guildhall, Preston. Losing to Steve Davis in the final, Terry nevertheless picked up the useful runner-up prize of £5000, plus £1000 as the scorer of the highest break – 131 against Tony Knowles. Steve Davis and Terry were again the finalists in the Lada Classic at Oldham, with Terry winning narrowly 9–8, and their next big clash was in the final of the Benson and Hedges Masters. This time it was Steve's turn to win, by 9 frames to 5. Their saga continued in the Yamaha Organs Trophy, Steve winning 9–7 in the final, and in the Benson and Hedges Irish Masters, where Terry triumphed over Steve, 9–5. When Steve Davis departed in the first round of the 1982 World Championship, Terry became the automatic favourite to take the title for the second time, yet a similar fate awaited the No. 3 seed when he was beaten, 10–6, by Willie Thorne – another first-round shock result! Terry is now down to fourteenth position in the world rankings list.

Alex Higgins

Alex learnt to play snooker in a Belfast billiard hall called The Jampot after being invited for a game by friends. He was ten years old. 'Within a few weeks I was making breaks of twenty and thirty and had left most of the lads behind. I was completely self-taught, but I soon got the feel of a cue and it was not long before I realised I had great natural ability.'

He won the Irish amateur title and after moving to Lancashire he entered the 1972 World Professional Championship. On his way to the Final against John Spencer, Alex, by now called 'Hurricane' Higgins, had to play in the qualifying rounds and defeated Ron Gross and Jack Rea. Into the quarter-finals, he beat John Pulman 31–23 and won by the odd frame in the semi-finals against Rex Williams 31–30. His victory over Spencer in Birmingham was achieved by 37 frames to 32 and Higgins, at the age of 22, became the youngest title-holder in snooker history.

Higgins was invited to play in the 1973 *Pot Black* series and obliged his followers in the first programme with a break of 60, beating John Pulman 101–50. However, the title of *Pot Black* Champion eluded him and he was beaten by Rex Williams, Jack Rea and Fred Davis.

On his way to the final of the 1976 World Championship Alex had narrowly defeated Cliff Thorburn, John Spencer and Eddie Charlton. In the 53-frame final, however, Ray Reardon was at his best, winning 27–16. Revenge for Higgins came at Leeds shortly after when he beat Reardon for the £1000 first prize in the Canadian Club Tournament.

Alex was knocked out in the first round of the 1977 World Championship by Doug Mountjoy, the 1978 *Pot Black* Champion. The winning margin was a solitary frame, 13–12, and the match was decided on the last black of the 25th frame. History repeated itself, unluckily for Alex, when in the 1978 World Championship he played and lost against Patsy Fagan with the scores again at 13–12. Alex, who had defeated Dennis Taylor to retain his Irish Professional title, successfully met another challenge from Dubliner, Patsy Fagan, in 1978. The game was held at the Ulster Hall, Belfast, with Higgins winning by 21 frames to 13. He also won the 1977 Canadian Open Championship beating John Spencer by 17 to 14 at the National Exhibition Centre at Toronto. Playing in the 1978 *Pot Black* series, his second appearance, Alex lost to Dennis Taylor and Doug Mountjoy. His one victory, over Ray Reardon by 90 to 53, included a 50 break which took Alex just three minutes!

One of his best triumphs in 1978 came in the Benson and Hedges Masters at the New London Theatre, Drury Lane. He won 4–3 in the quarter-finals against Dennis Taylor, and then heavily defeated Ray Reardon 5–1 in the semi-finals. The other finalist, Cliff Thorburn, had previously beaten Doug Mountjoy and John Spencer. The result was a victory for Alex 7–5, and a cheque for £3000. He surprisingly lost to David Taylor in the semi-finals of the UK Professional Championship later in the year, and also to the young Tony Meo in the semi-finals of the Canadian Open Championship at Toronto.

Early in 1979 Alex experienced yet another semi-final defeat, this time by Graham Miles in the Holsten Lager Tournament. His game against Terry Griffiths in the 1979 World Championship was one of the highlights of the entire tournament. Their quarter-final encounter resulted in a win for Griffiths in the final frame with the scores level at 12 frames each! As one of the UK challengers for the

1979 Canadian International at Toronto, having beaten two other Canadians, Alex played Cliff Thorburn in the semi-finals but lost 9–6.

1980 was a busy year for Alex with some 'hits' and very near misses. He lost his Irish Professional title to Dennis Taylor in a match played at the Ulster Hall, Belfast, by 21 frames to 15, and was runner-up to John Spencer in the Wilson's Classic and to Terry Griffiths in the Benson and Hedges Masters. His major successes, however, came in the Tolly Cobbold, the Padmore/Super Crystalate International (against Perrie Mans), and the British Gold Cup, in which he beat Ray Reardon in the final. He got to within two frames of becoming the World Champion for the second time when he lost to Cliff Thorburn in the 1980 Final by 18 frames to 16.

Enjoying the somewhat more relaxed atmosphere of Pontin's holiday village at Camber Sands a few days later, Alex won the professional competition, beating Dennis Taylor 9–7. At Toronto in September he lost to Terry Griffiths in the semi-finals of the Canadian Open, and failed by 16 frames to 6 against Steve Davis in the final of the Coral UK at Preston Guildhall in November. He played in *Pot Black* 81 but only took one frame out of three in the qualifying round.

The Irishman's winning streak returned in January 1981 at the Wembley Conference Hall with the £6000 first prize in the Benson and Hedges Masters, beating Cliff Thorburn in the semi-finals and Terry Griffiths in the final. Oddly enough, in the Benson and Hedges 'Irish' Masters Alex lost in the semi-finals to Welshman Ray Reardon! In January 1981 the 'Hurricane' became the third snooker professional as the 'subject' on *This Is Your Life*, but his appearance in the World Snooker Championship, where he was seeded four, was limited to one round in which he lost to Steve Davis, 13–8. He later blamed too busy an engagement diary prior to the tournament for his loss of form and 'sparkle'.

Although Alex lost two 'good conduct' marks after the 1981 World Championship, dropping to eleventh place in the world ratings, he returned in triumph to the 1982 event at the Crucible Theatre, Sheffield. Playing his best snooker for nearly a decade, Alex defeated a formidable succession of opponents – Jim Meadowcroft, Doug Mountjoy, Willie Thorne, Jimmy White, and finally Ray

Reardon – to become World Champion for the second time. Meanwhile Alex had competed in *Pot Black* 82, winning just one game, against Cliff Thorburn. Alex goes into the 1983 season ranked second.

Tony Knowles

Now in his late twenties, Tony, who comes from Bolton, has been playing snooker since the age of nine. His father was a steward at the Tonge Moor Conservative Club where the young Tony managed to practise on the club's full-sized table. He was a proficient player by the age of sixteen and met and played his idol, Alex Higgins, in occasional exhibition matches. Tony went to art college where he qualified as a graphic artist but upon leaving at the age of eighteen he decided upon a full-time snooker career. He won the British Junior (Under 19) Championship twice – in 1972 and 1974 – and later represented England in Home International Team matches. He was the 'hero' of the winning England side in 1979, losing only two frames out of fifteen and receiving the 'Player of the Series' Award. He first had individual successes also in 1979, winning three important amateur tournaments including a £1000 first prize in the Pontin's autumn festival.

Tony turned professional at the beginning of 1980 but was too late to qualify for that year's World Championship. After a patient year of waiting and exhibition matches, Tony entered his first World Championship in 1981 but was knocked out, 10–8, in the first round by Graham Miles. He at last achieved a modest triumph and public recognition during the TV transmissions from the Coral UK Professional Championship at Preston. His 9–6 defeat of Doug Mountjoy and subsequent own defeat by 9–5 against Terry Griffiths in the quarter-finals were seen by millions of viewers, thus partially answering Tony's previous complaint: 'What I need is some television exposure'.

And there was to be more. Tony started the 1982 World Championship as a 150-1 'outsider', having to win his qualifying game against Eugene Hughes (Dublin) to reach the first round. The first session of the first round found Tony drawn against the defending champion,

Steve Davis, the odds-on favourite. Davis, inexplicably, was completely off form, and again millions of viewers watched with disbelief as Tony Knowles defeated him by 10 frames to 1. It was a well-deserved win for Tony, who played with confidence and skill throughout. He went on to take his second-round match, 13–7, from Graham Miles but, in the quarter-finals for the first time in his career, eventually lost, 13–11, to Eddie Charlton. He was later selected as a member of the England team in the 1982 State Express Team Classic, and is ranked fifteenth for the 1983 season, which began well for him when he defeated David Taylor, 6–3, in the final of the Jameson Whiskey International, his first major tournament. His cheque for £22,000 (plus £1500 for the highest break) was the highest individual prize outside the World Championship.

Perrie Mans

The South African Snooker Champion from Johannesburg was invited to make his first appearance in *Pot Black* for the 1977 series. Perrie, whose actual name is Pierre, was one of the less fancied players in a line-up which included eleven other top-class professionals. His first game was against veteran Fred Davis which Perrie won by

66 points to 48. Next he beat Ray Reardon by 88 points to 42 and then Willie Thorne by 89 points to 42. It was now obvious that Perrie had taken the opportunity to become the first South African *Pot Black* Champion very seriously! Having now reached the Final, his opponent was another newcomer to the series, the Welsh player Doug Mountjoy. Showing almost complete indifference both to the television cameras and his rival, Perrie's determination to win was reflected in the result – Mans 90, Mountjoy 21. Perrie's score of 90 included a break of 59, the highest of the 1977 series.

One of the few left-handed players, Perrie had reached the quarter-finals of the 1974 World Championship by beating John Spencer. He defeated Graham Miles to reach the semi-finals in 1976 but, at Sheffield in 1977,

Perrie was unable to survive the first round, losing to Dennis Taylor by 13–11. It was a different story when he returned to the Crucible Theatre one year later for, en route to the Final, he defeated the current World Champion John Spencer by 13 frames to 8. Perrie's next victim was Graham Miles 13–7, followed by a victory over Fred Davis in the semi-finals with the score at 18–16.

The marathon Final, watched by millions of *Grandstand* viewers, was against Ray Reardon, and although Perrie led at one stage by 18 frames to 17 he then succumbed to the Welshman's superior skill and experience. Perrie had to be content with the runner-up prize with the final score Reardon 25, Mans 18.

Perrie returned to the 1979 *Pot Black* team to retrieve the Trophy he had won in 1977. His first three games, against Doug Mountjoy, Fred Davis and Steve Davis, were all won convincingly and Perrie proceeded to the semi-finals without having lost a frame in two series! But here his run came to an end when his opponent in the 1978 World Championship Final, Ray Reardon, won 78–41. After an unsuccessful first round in the Holsten Lager International, Perrie's next major tournament was the Benson and Hedges Masters, held at the Wembley Conference Centre. In turn he defeated Cliff Thorburn, Ray Reardon and, in the Final, Alex Higgins to take the £3000 first prize.

The 1979 World Championship at Sheffield, in which Perrie was the number two seed, ended in the first round, when he lost to the eventual champion, Terry Griffiths, 8–13.

Snooker exists in South Africa mainly as an amateur sport. Until recently, Perrie has been offered little match-play experience or opposition in his own country. The situation has now dramatically changed since more of his fellow countrymen have been accepted into the professional ranks. In 1979 Jimmy van Rensburg, Derek Mienie and Roy Amdor became professionals with the almost immediate result of Perrie losing his South African Champion's title! He was beaten, 9–3, in the semi-finals by Mienie, who then defeated van Rensburg in the final, 9–6.

Perrie was a member of the unsuccessful 'Rest of the World' team for the State Express World Cup in the autumn of 1979 and later returned to the Midlands to compete in his third *Pot Black* series, where one win, against Doug Mountjoy, was not enough for him to reach the semi-finals. But Perrie's next tournament was more rewarding when he gained £1000 as the runner-up to Alex Higgins in the final of the Padmore/Super Crystalate International.

The next time that these two players met was in the Benson and Hedges Masters at Wembley Conference Centre, with Higgins winning again, by 5 frames to 1. In the 1980 World Championship, Perrie was seeded number eight and his first game in the second round was, unfortunately for the South African, against – Alex Higgins! The result was a further win for Higgins by 13 frames to 6. Seeded 7 in the 1981 World Championship, Perrie again exited in the second round by a margin of 13 frames to 5 against 'Big' Bill Werbeniuk. He had previously scored a slightly unexpected success, beating Steve Davis 5–3 in the first round of the Benson and Hedges Masters, but his quarter-final game was a 5–4 failure against Cliff Thorburn.

Perrie's position in the 1982 world ranking list dropped to 15. In the World Championship his first-round game resulted in a narrow victory, 10–8. against the unseeded Tony Meo, followed by a 13–6 defeat when he met Jimmy White in the second. In his only other major tournament, the Jameson Whiskey, Perrie went out in the third round, 5–3, against Steve Davis, previously beating Tony Meo once more by the same score in the second round. Perrie is now ranked eleventh for the 1983 season.

Tony Meo

The 1978 Junior Snooker Champion, christened Anthony Christian Meo by his Italian parents, was born in London in October 1959. Tony began to show signs of obvious ability at snooker when he started to play the game at the age of thirteen. 'After a year or so,' he says, 'people told me that I should take it up seriously.' Which is what Tony did, and by 1977 he had won several amateur championships, including the Tirfor and the Warner's Pro-Am.

The last few years have seen Tony really make his presence felt on the snooker circuit. At Prestatyn in May
1978 he was narrowly beaten by Steve Davis in the

Pontin's Open Championship 7–6. At Leeds he took the title of Junior Snooker Champion from Ian Williamson, who had held it for two years. His outstanding performance of the year, however, was in Toronto, Canada, when he competed in the Canadian Open Championship and won his way into the Final against Cliff Thorburn, having defeated Alex Higgins in the semi-finals. Although Meo lost 17–15, he showed that he is one of the most promising young players in the country. He was runner-up to Mike Hallett of Grimsby in the 'Pot Red' tournament at Wembley in December 1978, which featured eight of the top teenage snooker players. He reached the quarter-finals of the English Amateur Snooker Championship (Southern Section) in 1979 but did not reproduce his best form on this occasion, losing 4–2.

At the age of 17 Tony was the youngest player ever to score a 147 break – against Terry Whitthread at the Pot Black Snooker Centre in Clapham. In the summer of 1979 he set up another record by being accepted as a professional player at the age of nineteen. One of his first major tournaments was the 1979 Coral UK, where he beat Manchester's David Taylor by 9–7 before losing to the eventual champion, John Virgo. In the British Gold Cup he defeated Steve Davis, Roy Andrewartha and Doug

89

Mountjoy before losing to Alex Higgins in the semi-finals. Tony had to qualify from 'scratch' in the 1980 World Championship which he did with an impressive win over Jimmy van Rensburg (South Africa) by 9 frames to 1. His first-round game was one of his best performances so far, losing by just one frame, 10–9, to Alex Higgins.

The 1980 Coral UK ended for Tony in the quarter-finals where he lost 9–5 to Steve Davis, who also beat him 9–3 in the final of the John Courage English Professional Championship. Tony was also going strong in the 1981 World Championship, where he made a break of 134 against John Virgo in the first round, winning 10 frames to 6, before he met Terry Griffiths in the second round, losing by 13–6.

Tony beat Alex Higgins, 6–1, in the final of the 1981 Lucania Professional Championship, and in Australia he won the Winfield Masters – their television equivalent to *Pot Black*. In the 1982 Benson and Hedges Masters he beat David Taylor and Cliff Thorburn, earning a place in the semi-finals. Although he lost to his stable-mate, Steve Davis, he had the distinction of scoring the highest break in the competition – 136.

Starting as the eighteenth seed for the 1982 World Championship, Tony lost to Perrie Mans, 10–8, in the first round but is probably a much better player than his 24th position in the 1982 world ranking list suggests. He still has ample time to consolidate his earlier promising form.

Graham Miles

Birmingham's own snooker star made a quiet but effective entry into the professional scene. Graham had won several minor tournaments in the Midlands but he really came to prominence in 1973 when he reached the World Championship quarter-finals before losing to Eddie Charlton. However, this performance and a growing public reputation led to Miles being invited to play in the 1974 series of *Pot Black*. In the three-frame Final, Graham won against John Spencer by taking the first two frames and scoring the highest break in the competition. A few weeks later he maintained this form and reached the Final of the 1974 World Championship. On this occasion he was unable to cope with the opposition from Ray

Reardon who was defending his world title. He lost, 22–12, but had nearly brought off a remarkable 'double'.

The 1975 *Pot Black* competition once again included Graham and he proved that his previous success on the programme was no fluke. He defeated Ray Reardon in his first game by a large margin, then Eddie Charlton, before losing to John Spencer. These victories were sufficient to get himself into the semi-finals where he had a narrow win over Reardon. The Final against Dennis Taylor saw Graham the *Pot Black* Champion for the second year in succession.

Pot Black 1978 celebrated its tenth year on BBC-2 and

Graham was undefeated until he met Doug Mountjoy in the Final. He took the first frame but with Doug in superlative form the Midlander finished as runner-up. Twelve months later these two players met yet again in the first semi-final of *Pot Black* 1979. Graham had won against Eddie Charlton and John Spencer to improve his chances of winning the Championship for the third time. Mountjoy ended his hopes by taking the game by 77 points to 40 with Graham gracious in defeat. It was this sporting spirit displayed by Miles which contributed to the decision to present him with the *Pot Black* personality award at the end of the series. He later competed in an invitation tournament at the Bombay Gymkhana taking the third prize with victories over Patsy Fagan and Dennis Taylor. The Midlander lost to Ray Reardon in the first round of the 1979 World Championship – a game where he was handicapped by a severe attack of flu.

Graham, who is the manager of a building company in Birmingham, has always been known for his unorthodox style of 'sighting' with the cue rubbing the left-hand side of his chin. It is believed that he is now trying to change his stance to a more conventional method. Meanwhile, the old style has produced two maximum breaks of 147 and in the 1978 UK Championship he scored a break of 139, a record for the event.

Graham's name didn't figure too prominently in the results lists of 1980's important tournaments. He represented England in the State Express World Cup where his team was beaten in the Final by Wales, Graham losing to Terry Griffiths and Doug Mountjoy. In *Pot Black* 80 his one success was over Perrie Mans by 93 points to 18, when he cleared the table with a magnificent break of 68. But he was disappointing in the Padmore/Super Crystalate International against Willie Thorne and against John Spencer in the Wilson's Classic; a 9–5 defeat by Patsy Fagan put him out of the Coral UK, and he made an early exit from the British Gold Cup in a Group 3 play-off against Tony Meo. His fortunes were no better in the 1980 World Championship, suffering another defeat, 10–3, by the young Canadian Kirk Stevens in the first round.

During the 1980–1 season Graham's programme included the Champion of Champions where he beat Alex Higgins 5–4 but failed to qualify in his group. He lost to Eddie Sinclair (Glasgow) in the first round of the Coral

UK, and to Cliff Thorburn in the second round of the World Championship. But a much overdue success materialised for the Midlander in the Tolly Cobbold Classic in February 1981, when Graham produced his best form for some time to score a convincing win against Cliff Thorburn in the final by 5 frames to 1 and take the £2000 first prize.

No other major prizes have come Graham's way since, although he got to the Tolly Cobbold semi-finals again in 1982, losing to Steve Davis on this occasion. He competed in the Yamaha Organs and again went out in the Group B semi-finals. His form in the 1982 World Championship was only moderate and, after a first round win over Dave Martin, he was beaten, 13–7, by Tony Knowles, fresh from his victory over Steve Davis. Ranked 16 in 1981, Graham is now down to 18.

Doug Mountjoy

Doug's snooker career from his amateur days to joining the professional ranks bears a strong resemblance to that of his fellow Welshman, Ray Reardon. Both are ex-miners and former Welsh Amateur Snooker Champions. Doug's name first appeared in the record books in 1966 as the runner-up for the Welsh Amateur Championship. He won the title in 1968 and again in 1976. During this period he also represented Wales in the International Tournaments and won against Patsy Fagan (Ireland) and John Virgo (England). The World Amateur Snooker Championship was held at the President Hotel, Johannesburg, in October 1976 with some of the games shown on the new South African television service. Twenty-four players competed and Doug, playing in Group One, won all his seven games and fought his way to the Final. His opponent, Paul Mifsud from Malta, managed to win just one frame out of twelve!

The new World Amateur Champion was then invited to play in *Pot Black* and Mountjoy decided to turn professional. His first appearance in *Pot Black* saw him reach the 1977 Final, but he was given little chance by Perrie Mans. Nevertheless, Doug had justified his inclusion in the series and was satisfied with his decision to become a professional.

This confidence and optimism was confirmed when, in early 1977, Doug met his Welsh colleague Ray Reardon in the Final of the Benson and Hedges Masters Tournament at the London Theatre, Drury Lane. Doug had already beaten John Pulman, Fred Davis and Alex 'Hurricane' Higgins to qualify and he went on to further victory with a 7 frames to 6 win against Reardon. Later that year Doug was knocked out in the quarter-finals of the World Championship by Dennis Taylor, and in 1978 lost to Ray Reardon in the first round.

Meanwhile, Doug had played again in his second *Pot Black*, losing to Ray Reardon but winning against Alex Higgins and Dennis Taylor. He was then in the Final for the second year running, and won two of the three frames against Graham Miles, including the highest break of 101, earning the title of *Pot Black* Champion 1978.

Only a few weeks before returning to the *Pot Black* studios to defend his title in the 1979 series, he competed in the UK Professional Championship at the Guild Hall, Preston. The Tournament, sponsored by Corals, saw Doug defeat Dennis Taylor, Roy Andrewartha, Graham Miles and (in the Final) David Taylor, to achieve yet another important snooker honour. The new UK Champion then played in his third series of *Pot Black*. With victories over Steve Davis and Graham Miles he reached the Final for the third year in succession. On this occasion fellow Welshman, Ray Reardon, beat him 2–1. Mountjoy, however, once again won the Highest Break prize and the Joe Davis Trophy with a score of 82.

Doug subsequently took his revenge when he defeated Reardon in the Final of the Benson and Hedges Masters Tournament played in Ireland. Although unseeded, he was one of the more fancied players to win the 1979 World Championship at Sheffield. However, after winning his two qualifying matches Doug lost to Eddie Charlton in the first round. The next major competition for Doug was held at the scene of some of his earlier triumphs, the Pontin's Snooker Festival at Prestatyn. Doug had, as an amateur, twice won the Pontin's Open, and on this occasion, playing against his professional colleagues, he emerged the winner in the Final against Graham Miles. Later in 1979 he was a member of a formidable Welsh Trio in the State Express World Challenge Cup. With Terry Griffiths and Ray Reardon, he

formed an unbeatable combination which defeated England in the Final, sharing the first prize of £7500.

Doug's attempt to win the Coral UK title for the second year running ended in the second round when he lost to Steve Davis by 9 frames to 5. The Woodpecker Welsh Professional Championship, held at the Leisure Centre in his home-town of Ebbw Vale, featured Doug, Ray Reardon, Terry Griffiths and Cliff Wilson. It was a triumph for Doug with victories over Terry Griffiths and then the title-holder, Ray Reardon, in the Final. He therefore approached the 1980 World Championship with a certain degree of confidence, having beaten the 1978 and 1979 World Champions! His first opponent was Cliff Wilson, whom he beat by 10 frames to 6. He then found himself drawn against the eventual winner, Cliff Thorburn, in the next round. This game resulted in a 13–10 defeat after Doug had levelled the score at 10–10 at one stage, making a break of 123 in the last session. In *Pot Black* 80 Doug reached the semi-finals yet again, but was beaten by Ray Reardon. In the 'play-off' with Dennis Taylor, Doug won to earn a third place in the competition.

The New London Theatre, Drury Lane, London, was the setting for two of Doug's successes in the autumn of 1980. In October he won the title of 'Champion of Champions' after a round-robin contest in which he defeated John Virgo in the Final by 10 frames to 8. Then within a fortnight, together with Ray Reardon and Terry Griffiths he comprised the Welsh team which won the State Express World Cup for the second year in succession. Doug's own moments of glory, though, were to be in the 1981 World Championship at Sheffield. His break of 145 against Ray Reardon in the semi-finals earned him £1200 for the highest break in the tournament plus £5000 for the record break in the history of the Championship. Seeded 14, he fought his way to the final with victories against Willie Thorne, Eddie Charlton, Dennis Taylor and Ray Reardon. Doug's ultimate disappointment, losing 18–12 to Steve Davis, was at least partially compensated by the additional £10,000 he received as the runner-up.

The 1981–2 season continued as busily as ever for Doug – the Jameson International, where he suffered a 5–1 defeat by Alex Higgins in the third round; the Coral UK, beaten by Tony Knowles, 9–6, also in the third round; the Northern Ireland Classic, losing 9–8 to Jimmy White in the semi-finals; and of course *Pot Black* 82. After being a 'group loser' in the Yamaha Organs Trophy, Doug put in some hard practice, which paid rapid dividends – £5000 as the winner of the Woodpecker Welsh Professional Championship, his second success in this competition in three years. Next was the 1982 World Championship, where he first beat Rex Williams comfortably, 10–3, then lost to Alex Higgins in the second round by the narrowest of margins – 13–12. Doug is now seventh in the current rankings list.

John Pulman

The World Professional Snooker Champion from 1957 to 1968 was born in Devon. He made his first billiards century at the age of twelve and won the English Amateur Championship in 1946. This was also the year that he decided to turn professional, winning £400 in his first major tournament. John was now entitled to compete against the 'giants' of snooker, Joe Davis and his brother Fred, and the Scottish World Champion, Walter Donaldson, on level terms.

The six foot two bespectacled Devonian reached the finals of the World Championships in 1955 and 1956, losing on both occasions to Fred Davis. In 1957, however, John won his first World title against Irishman Jack Rea. There were no further World contests until 1964, but then John successfully defended his title each year up to 1968. His opponents had included Fred Davis, Rex Williams and Eddie Charlton. Pulman was runner-up to Ray Reardon in 1970 but made no great impact in the World Championship again until 1977, when he lost to the eventual Champion, John Spencer, in the semi-finals by only two frames.

One of the original members of the *Pot Black* team in 1969, John has appeared on the programme many times. In October 1972 he was seriously hurt in a car crash but

recovered in time to play in the 1973 series in December and to succeed against his old rivals Rex Williams and Fred Davis. John's recent tilts at the tournament windmills have proved mainly unsuccessful. His knowledge and experience of the game, however, have been used in a new role – that of commentator. His voice has been heard on *Pot Black* and, after having been knocked out of the 1979 World Championship in an early round, he swopped his cue for a microphone and joined the BBC commentary team at Sheffield for the remainder of the competition. This occurrence was repeated in the 1980 World Championship after losing to Jim Wych and in 1981 after a very early exit against Dave Martin, a new professional, in the qualifying rounds.

Following a leg injury after being knocked down by a bus, John's playing career has been even more severely curtailed. He has recently signed a contract as a television snooker commentator with a commercial channel, and has been the resident coach at a London snooker centre.

Ray Reardon

The 1978 World Professional Snooker Champion was born in Tredegar, South Wales, on 8 October 1932. The young Ray inherited his love of snooker from his father and his uncles, all miners, and at the age of 14 he too was working in the pits. Reardon became the Welsh Amateur Snooker Champion in 1950 and held this title until 1956.

After a near-fatal pit accident, he eventually left the mining industry and joined the Stoke-on-Trent Constabulary. He quickly established himself as the Police Snooker Champion and went on to win the English Amateur Championship from another famous player – John Spencer.

Turning professional, Reardon held the World Championship from April to November 1970. In the 75-frame final at the City Hall, Manchester, in April 1973 he beat Eddie Charlton to win the Championship for the second time. Just twelve months later, back in Manchester at Belle Vue, he won his third title with a comparatively easy victory over the 1974 *Pot Black* Champion, Graham Miles, by 22–12.

The 1975 World Championship, played in Australia,

extended Reardon to the full and this time it was no easy win for him. In the Final against Eddie Charlton in Sydney Ray won by just one frame! In 1976, however, back in Manchester he won his fifth title comparatively easily.

The 1977 World Championship was staged at the Crucible Theatre in Sheffield. Reardon won his first-round match against Patsy Fagan comfortably enough by 13 frames to 7 but in the quarter-finals the defending champion met John Spencer and, obviously nowhere near his best form, was beaten 13 frames to 6.

His return to glory took just twelve months and at the same venue. He regained the World title, his sixth, beating the Australian Eddie Charlton in the semi-finals and South African Perrie Mans in the Final.

With the exception of 1971, when Reardon was touring South Africa, he has competed in every *Pot Black* series to date and won the first Trophy in 1969. He was the losing finalist in 1970 and 1972, and in 1975 he beat Fred Davis in the 'play-off' for the special prize for third place in the tournament.

One of Ray's major successes in 1978 was in the *Daily*

Mirror 'Champion of Champions' Tournament at the Wembley Conference Centre, where he beat Alex Higgins, 11–9, to win the first prize of £2000. Ray carried this form forward shortly after to the recordings of the 1979 *Pot Black* competition. He won his first game against John Spencer, lost to Eddie Charlton and then defeated Graham Miles, Perrie Mans and Doug Mountjoy to become *Pot Black* Champion for the second time.

Ray's downfall brought about by Dennis Taylor in the quarter-finals of the 1979 World Championship was the biggest upset of the tournament. The reigning World Champion had started, as number one seed, a warm favourite to win the title for the seventh time. His first game, against Graham Miles, was won comfortably enough, 13–8, but a seeming loss of concentration in the quarter-finals contributed to his departure from the championship stakes with Dennis Taylor winning this time also 13–8.

Ray shared the first prize with Terry Griffiths and Doug Mountjoy when Wales won the State Express World Challenge Cup at Haden Hill in the autumn of 1979. However, he was less pleased when a few weeks later Doug Mountjoy deprived him of the Welsh Professional Champion title at Ebbw Vale! His eleventh appearance in *Pot Black* 80 began well, with three wins in a row against Terry Griffiths, John Spencer and Dennis Taylor. With a further win against Doug Mountjoy in the semi-finals Ray was in the *Pot Black* Final once again, where his opponent was his old rival Eddie Charlton, who lost the first frame but took the next two leaving Ray with the runner-up prize for the third time in the programme's history.

Reardon's next main events were the Benson and Hedges Masters, where he lost to Alex Higgins in the semi-finals, and the 1980 World Championship. The six-times winner started favourite and kept his supporters happy, winning his first game against Bill Werbeniuk by 13 frames to 6. One of the biggest upsets of the tournament occurred in the quarter-finals, however, when David Taylor (a 66–1 outsider) put the ex-Champion out of the competition with a 13–11 victory.

The next twelve months were as busy as ever for Ray. He played in *Pot Black* 81 – his twelfth appearance in the series – and was unbeaten in his first three games against

Cliff Thorburn, Steve Davis and Kirk Stevens, but lost to Jim Wych in the semi-finals and, eventually, to Eddie Charlton in the 'Play-Off' for third place in the competition. However, a major tournament that he did succeed in winning was the Woodpecker Welsh Professional Championship in February 1981 where he regained his title from Terry Griffiths and Cliff Wilson. Ray had previously, of course, represented the Welsh Team (with Terry Griffiths and Doug Mountjoy) which won the State Express World Cup in October 1980. In the 1981 World Championship itself, the former Champion again reached the semi-finals after scoring against John Spencer and Bill Werbeniuk. There his fellow countryman, Doug Mountjoy, inflicted a 16–10 defeat on Ray during which Doug made a break of 145!

Ray, one of the busiest and most consistent professionals, was presented with the *Pot Black* Personality Award at the end of the 1982 series. He won the Highland Masters at the Eden Court Theatre, Inverness, in April 1982 with a 6–0 victory over Steve Davis in the semi-finals and by 11–4 against John Spencer in the Final. His most notable achievement of the year was in reaching the final of the 1982 World Championship, where he lost to Alex Higgins by 18 frames to 15. Nevertheless Ray's record over the last three World Championships earns him the number one placing for the 1983 event.

Ray lives at Werrington, Stoke-on-Trent, and was the first snooker player to be featured on *This Is Your Life*, in 1976. He has made many radio and television appearances since then and, when time permits, is to be found perfecting his potting (*sic*!) on the golf course.

HOW TO BECOME A TOP PLAYER
by Ray Reardon

I have entered Championships both in England and Wales since the age of twelve. The first few years of participation in these events were purely to gain experience. Obviously, you always play to win; but at this age it is extremely useful to realise the feeling of playing before an audience. There is no substitute. Therefore, although winning is important, in losing you gain the drive to succeed the next time whilst learning to accept defeat gracefully.

To become a top player a great deal of sacrifice is

necessary. It means playing in all of your spare time. Always enjoy playing but learn from your mistakes and, better still, always take full advantage of your opponent's errors.

You will discover that basically snooker is a game of *memory*. To remember how you played a particular shot in the past will enable you to recognise it when it occurs again in a similar situation and you will know how to cope with it.

Practise as often as is possible, but not to the point of boredom. Take part in every tournament that is open to you. Set yourself a goal and when it is yours take the next step up the ladder until you reach the top. When your ambition is finally achieved *practise some more*!

Method of play

I have never set out to play any game in a certain way even when the form of my opponent is well known to me. This is because each and every frame of snooker is different. After all, when the frame has begun, sometimes the black ball and a minor colour have been placed in a safe position which could result in the game being played defensively. Always play your own style of game – do not try to beat your opponent at his game. You may consider yourself to be a better potter than him and play all-attacking snooker – this is not good. When you alter your own game you create flaws in your style and will become vulnerable.

Make your own game as sound as you can in all the departments of potting, safety play and the art of playing snookers. Become the master of the cue-ball and you will, more easily, realise your ambitions.

SNOOKER CLINIC
by Ray Reardon

The 'End Game' of snooker is vital and therefore it is imperative that you are sure of potting the remaining balls, when 'on'.

In order to tighten this part of your game, I strongly recommend that you practise the following 'Snooker Clinic' to perfection. When satisfied, place the white (cue) ball to your own chosen spot and practise.

Diagram 1

The cue-ball is set in the half-ball position to pot yellow ball into its own pocket. Strike the cue-ball at centre with enough strength to bring the cue-ball from the yellow ball onto the side cushion, then back into the centre of the table.

Diagram 2

Cue-ball is in a straight line with green ball. If we stop the cue-ball in place of green, a difficult shot on the brown follows. Therefore, cause the cue-ball to screw back a few inches to leave the brown ball easy. (Screw – this is done by striking the cue-ball three-quarters ball, which is between centre and table level, and sharp. Do not stab at the cue-ball, follow through with the cue.)

Diagram 3

This is an interesting shot, because we have three ways in which to play it and all three ways are correct.

'A' with deep screw, as described in Diagram 2, but played *very sharp*.

'B' again with screw, but this time with slight screw, so ease off with the sharpness.

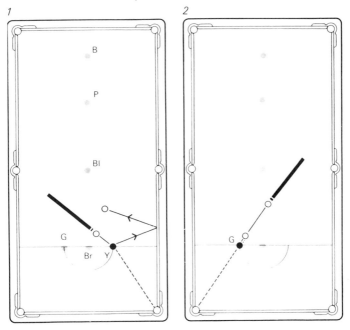

103

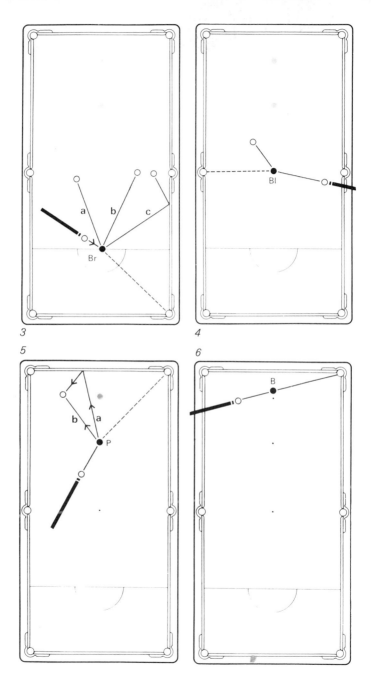

3

4

5

6

'C' – stun shot. Strike cue-ball just below centre firmly. This causes the cue-ball to bounce away from the brown ball on to the side cushion, then off again.

Diagram 4
Strike cue-ball at centre, nice and slow, which leaves natural position.

Diagram 5
Two ways. Either, 'A', strike cue-ball at centre and roll through on to cushion, then off again, or, 'B', use slight screw, as Diagram 3 at 'B'.

Diagram 6
Pot black the easy way. Remember, never mind how the black is potted, you can only win once, so make it easy. Nothing fancy, please – no exhibition stuff. Just be sure and win.

N.B. It will be noted that I have made no mention of the use of *side* when striking the cue-ball. This has been omitted intentionally, because its use can cause complications and the 'Clinic' is to assist the beginner.

Dean Reynolds

One of *Pot Black*'s Junior 'discoveries', Dean comes from Grimsby and was born in January 1963. He became interested in snooker at the age of five at his father's club, and began beating the senior members by the time he was twelve. In 1979 he won the Grimsby Boys Snooker Championship and the Lincs/South Humberside Junior Championship. By the end of 1980 Dean had made over fifty century breaks, including a personal best of 143.

His first appearance on television was in the 1981 series of *Junior Pot Black*, becoming the winner of the new trophy. He then went on to win the British Junior Under 19 Championship and turned professional in the autumn of 1981.

Playing in his first World Championship in 1982, the Junior Pot Black Champion put up a very creditable performance. He won his first two qualifying games against two experienced players – Dessie Sheehan (Dublin) and former World Amateur Champion Ray Edmonds (Cleethorpes). Dean then won his first round

match against the oldest and most experienced competitor in the tournament, Fred Davis, by 10 frames to 7. In the second round his opponent was the little-known South African Champion, Silvino Francisco, and Dean was not disgraced in losing by 13 frames to 8. A young man who should have a great future in snooker, Dean is ranked at 22 for the 1983 season.

John Spencer

Manchester's snooker star John Spencer learned to play at a local Sunday School Institute and made a break of 115 when he was just 15 years old. Three years later, after considerable dedication to the game, Spencer began his National Service. It was ten years before he took up snooker seriously again and after a succession of matches playing for side-stakes he entered the English Amateur Championships and lost narrowly in the Final to Ray Reardon.

He eventually gained this amateur title in 1966, turning professional in the same year. The 1969 *Pot Black* series included the new World Champion John Spencer amongst the more established star performers and he reached the Final, where his opponent was Ray Reardon. Spencer lost this game, but gained his revenge by beating Ray Reardon and Fred Davis in the 1970 and 1971 *Pot Black* Finals respectively.

Meanwhile, Spencer had won the World Championship again — in November 1970 — only to relinquish it to Alex Higgins in 1972. Spencer has often figured prominently in the closing stages of *Pot Black*. Apart from his successes in 1970 and 1971, he scored the highest break in 1972 and was runner-up to Graham Miles in 1974. In superb form throughout the 1976 series, John defeated Dennis Taylor in the Final to become the first 'three-time' winner of the *Pot Black* Trophy.

John was the local favourite to win the 1976 World Championship which was held at his home town of Manchester, but his quarter-final match against Alex Higgins ended disappointingly for him and his supporters when Higgins won by 15 frames to 14. The 1977 World Championship at Sheffield found John with renewed stamina and confidence. His path to winning the World title for the third time was paved with victories over John Virgo, Ray Reardon, John Pulman and, in the Final, the Canadian Cliff Thorburn. John was beaten by Perrie Mans in the first round of the 1978 contest, but not before he had scored the highest break of the Championship. The magnificent break of 138 was witnessed by millions of BBC-2 viewers.

John received the *Pot Black* 'Personality Award' in 1978 for being the only player to have appeared in ten series on the programme and to have won the *Pot Black* Trophy on three occasions. The 1979 *Pot Black* competition, however, proved to be an unlucky one for him, with just one win, against Eddie Charlton, to his credit. Spencer's winning streak returned within a short while when he won the Holsten Lager International at the Fulcrum Centre, Slough. In beating Graham Miles in the final 11–7 John clinched the first prize of £3500. It was during the quarter-finals that he scored a maximum break of 147 against Cliff Thorburn and earned another £500 from the sponsors. However, had he made this break in

107

another sponsored event the cheque would have been for
£10,000!

Later in the year John, together with some of his
colleagues, was invited to Bombay to compete in an
International 'Round-Robin' Tournament, sponsored by a
local paint company. At the finish John had won the first
prize (£2000), the Highest Break prize with a score of 108
and the Man of the Series award.

Back at the Crucible Theatre in Sheffield for the 1979
World Championship (and where he had won the title in
1977), John began the competition as the second
favourite. But he and his supporters were thwarted when

he lost to the burly Canadian Bill Werbeniuk in the first

round 13–11. The next twelve months were, with one exception, not particularly rewarding for John, although they were busy enough. He represented the English team (the runners-up) in the State Express World Cup and his other engagements included *Pot Black* 80, the Coral UK, the Padmore/Super Crystalate International, the British Gold Cup and the Benson and Hedges Masters. The former *Pot Black* Champion lost his three games in the 1980 series to Dennis Taylor, Ray Reardon and Terry Griffiths. It was Terry who also 'whitewashed' John, 5–0, in the Benson and Hedges semi-finals.

John's major success was in the brewery-sponsored Wilson's Classic at the New Century Hall, Manchester, in January 1980. His victims were Graham Miles, John Virgo and, in the final, Alex Higgins. John's 4–3 victory earned him the first prize of £3000 and it was his biggest financial gain since winning the Holsten Lager International the previous year. Following his defeat by Kirk Stevens, 13–8, in the 1980 World Championship he was placed in fifteenth position in the World Ranking List.

Between then and the 1981 World Championship John produced little of his winning form in major events. The nearest he came to the big prize money was in the Benson and Hedges Masters in January 1981, where he met Terry Griffiths in the semi-finals and at the end of a long, hard-fought game the score was 6–5 to Griffiths. This effort, nevertheless, was worth £2000 to John. He began the 1981 World Championship by narrowly defeating Ray Edmonds in the first round, 10–9, and then faced his old colleague and perennial opponent Ray Reardon. The result – Reardon 13, Spencer 11 – was an indication of both the pressure of the game on the two adversaries and how much John's previous form had returned.

Later that year Ray and John were again in opposition as members of the Wales and England teams in the State Express World Team Classic Final. It was John's turn to be on the winning side and to share the £12,000 prize money with Steve Davis and David Taylor. He played well below his best form in the 1982 World Championship, going out 13–5 against Willie Thorne in the second round, and continued the competition as one of the BBC commentary team! The former World Champion is now in twelfth place in the rankings list.

HOW TO WIN GAMES
by John Spencer

During my few years as a snooker professional travelling around the clubs, I have been asked a variety of questions about the game. I think the most interesting is why players who have been making 50–60 breaks frequently never seem to improve to the century-break class. I believe the answer to this is also one of the main differences between the professional and the top amateurs, and that is the mental attitude to the game. Obviously one of the reasons for this is that probably the professional has the ability to hold his concentration for long periods far better than most amateurs, but, this apart, it is reasonable to assume that a 60-break player can play most of the shots that a professional can play.

The basic mechanics of the game, once having been acquired, are only affected by one's own state of mind. Positive thinking produces positive play. As long as you think aggressively and positively you are mentally attuned to winning games, whereas if you continually think defensively, you are merely trying to avoid defeat.

A typical example of this attitude is shown when a player is left a longish straight red with all the other reds in a safe position. He will invariably get down and knock the red in nine times out of ten without even thinking. However, an identical shot with the remaining reds in such a position that his opponent will be left on if he misses the red will mean in some cases that he won't even attempt the red or miss the pot if he does. The reason for this is – he obviously isn't thinking positively; he is more concerned with what he is going to leave his opponent if he misses the pot and because of this his concentration is not entirely on the shot.

I think this attitude just about sums my game up. I have never been an admirer of the super tactician who, before a shot, weighs up all the possibilities and invariably prefers to wait for his opponent to make mistakes. Since I have been a professional I have always tried to be positive in my game, attacking whenever the opportunity arises. I don't believe in throwing my cue at everything in sight, but if, after weighing up the situation, I feel that it calls for aggression, I never hesitate. When I have made my mind up to go for a pot, I am concentrating a hundred per cent on the pot and never think what I will leave should I miss. Obviously, the amount of attacking a player does should depend on his own ability. Always play within your own limitations. If you are left a shot that you would normally knock in six times out of ten in practice, why refuse it because of the position of the other balls? After all, the percentage is that you will have six chances of winning to your opponent's four.

The best shots to go for are those which offer the maximum benefit when you get them and the least risk when you miss. The worst shots are those which offer the least benefit when you get them and the greatest risk when you miss. This is all part of the mental approach to the game, deciding when is the right time to attack.

Positive thinking also comes into safety play of course. Most players play a safety shot purely to stop their opponent from scoring, which can often be quite easy by running into the pyramid of reds, but this will leave your opponent a simple safety shot in return. Positive safety play is to try to put your opponent in the most awkward position from which to play a safety shot in return. Before playing your shot, study the position of the balls and decide the position that you would have most difficulty in escaping from, then try and put your opponent in the same spot.

Never begin a match with the thought that you have to win at all costs. This will put so much pressure on yourself that you will get tense even if things are going right for you and you won't be able to play your normal game. My own outlook is to play to the best of my ability and hope that it is good enough to win. Obviously I want to win as much as the next man, but I know it is not the end of the world if I lose. Believe it or not, I still get as much pleasure out of a game of snooker now as I did when I first started!

Kirk Stevens

'The Man in the White Suit' was one snooker columnist's description of Kirk Stevens, the young Canadian professional, when he appeared in the 1980 World Championship at Sheffield. He had, in fact, played in the same competition the year before without earning too much public recognition. Kirk was born in Toronto in August

1958. At the age of twelve he is said to have challenged Cliff Thorburn, then the resident professional at a billiard hall, to a game for two dollars! (Needless to add, Kirk lost.) Kirk, however, became a useful amateur player and in 1978 reached the semi-finals of the World Amateur Snooker Championship held in Malta. Although he was well beaten by Cliff Wilson, 8–2. he decided to turn professional and his application was accepted in December 1978. In 1979 he won back his two dollars (with interest), by defeating Cliff Thorburn, the reigning champion, by 7 frames to 5 for the Canadian Championship.

Kirk's first entry into the World Championship was also in 1979. He won his first two qualifying games against Roy Amdor (South Africa) and John Pulman and was then beaten by the veteran Fred Davis, 13–8, in the first round. Later he played for the Canadian team in the State Express World Cup where he beat Ray Reardon and Gary Owen, making a 69 break against Reardon. In September 1979 he was home in Toronto for the Canadian International, beating Dennis Taylor in the quarter-finals and losing by one frame, 9–8, to Terry Griffiths in the semis.

The inaugural Canadian Professional Championship, sponsored by Dufferin Cues, was held in April 1980 when Kirk was beaten by his young contemporary, Jim Wych, 9–7 in the semi-finals. His second appearance in the World Championship, however, really brought him to the notice of the public, press and television viewers alike. He started quietly but successfully, with wins in the qualifying section over David Greaves and Mike Hallett. His first-round game was a decisive defeat of Graham Miles by 10 frames to 3, in which Kirk had a break of 136, tying with Steve Davis for the highest break in the Championship. In the second round the Canadian performed another 'giant-killing' act, disposing of John Spencer 13–8 with breaks of 91 and 88. His quarter-final game was against Eddie Charlton and, with a confident win by 13 frames to 7, Kirk Stevens became the youngest player ever to enter the semi-finals. Kirk, whose style is similar at times to that of Alex Higgins, was now facing the 'Hurricane' himself and led 5–2 at the first interval, but gradually the strain of having played so many frames in a concentrated few days began to tell, and Higgins drew ahead to win by 16 frames to 13.

By now Kirk's cheerful personality and talent had scored a hit with the British snooker-loving public and he was subsequently invited to play in *Pot Black* 81. He beat Steve Davis in his first game, but then lost to Cliff Thorburn and Ray Reardon. However, he did not leave the competition empty-handed, for during his game against Steve Davis his break of 79 won him the prize for the highest break in the series. The 1981 World Championship was not so fortuitous for Kirk where he lost his second-round match against Dennis Taylor, 13–11, after winning 10–4 against John Dunning. Kirk was a losing semi-finalist to David Taylor in the Yamaha Organs Trophy at Derby and a losing quarter-finalist to Terry Griffiths in the Benson and Hedges Irish Masters, Dublin. As a member of the Canadian team for the 1980 State Express World Cup, Kirk again was on the losing side when Wales beat Canada in the Final.

Before the 1982 World Championship Kirk played little snooker and won less. He represented Canada again in the World Team Classic, together with Cliff Thorburn and Bill Werbeniuk, but his side lost to England in the semi-finals. He was beaten 5–0 by David Taylor in the third round of the Jameson and by Werbeniuk, 9–7, in the Coral UK. Kirk reproduced something near his best form at the

113

Crucible Theatre, where he reached the quarter-finals of the 1982 World Championship. Seeded No. 10, the young Canadian was beaten 13–9 by the younger Londoner, Jimmy White, after wins against Jack Fitzmaurice and Patsy Fagan in the earlier rounds. Kirk's performances in the premier event have earned him sixth place in the world rankings.

David Taylor

Another player born, bred and based in Manchester, in 1968 David Taylor won both the English Amateur Snooker Championship and the World Amateur Championship, held in Melbourne. It was not surprising that these feats prompted him to turn professional later that year. He was a member of the 1971 *Pot Black* team but, for a large part of his professional career, has enjoyed only moderate success on the tournament circuit. All his previous form was exceeded in the 1978 UK Championship at Preston where he started as one of the less fancied 'runners' and caused the major surprise of the competition by defeating Patsy Fagan, John Virgo and Alex Higgins before losing to Doug Mountjoy in the final. In June 1978, he made three consecutive clearances with breaks of 130, 140 and 139 at Butlin's, Minehead; this is now recognised as a world record.

David's performances in the World Professional Championships until the spring of 1980 were modest, although he had twice reached the quarter-finals. He lost in the first round of the 1979 event to Alex Higgins, but 1980 was a different story. An easy win in the first round over Ray Edmonds (another former World Amateur Champion) was followed by a 13–5 victory against Fred Davis. Once again David was in the quarter-finals and facing the formidable opposition of the favourite, six-times World Champion Ray Reardon. Playing his best snooker for some years, David effected yet another reversal of form which resulted in his winning by 13 frames to 11. He was not disgraced in losing, in the semi-finals, to the eventual World Champion of 1980, Cliff Thorburn. David thus 'jumped' from fifteenth to ninth position in the World Rankings list, but, after the 1981 World Championship where he reached the quarter-finals (losing to Cliff

Thorburn again), he was ranked No. 7. David returned to *Pot Black* 81 after an absence of some ten years, but only succeeded in winning one of his three qualifying frames. A few weeks later, though, the 'Silver Fox' was at his peak again and beat all but Steve Davis in the newly sponsored Yamaha Organs Trophy. As runner-up he collected £5000 and the satisfaction of having beaten Doug Mountjoy, Graham Miles and Kirk Stevens en route.

A member of the victorious trio (with Steve Davis and John Spencer) who won the 1982 World Team Classic, David also played in *Pot Black* 82, beating Alex Higgins but not qualifying for the semi-finals. He lost in the Group B semi-finals in the Yamaha Trophy, having previously beaten Cliff Thorburn, Alex Higgins and Tony Meo, and, surprisingly, failed against Patsy Fagan in the first round of the 1982 World Championship. He is seeded eighth in the current ranking list.

Dennis Taylor

Dennis Taylor was invited to join the 1975 *Pot Black* team after his promising form both here and in Canada. At the age of 25 he was the youngest member of the team.

He learned to play the game in Coalisland, County Tyrone, and arrived in Darwen, Lancs, at the age of 17. He won the British Junior Billiards title in 1968 and is now recognised as one of the most promising young professionals. Dennis lives in Blackburn and is married with two children.

In September 1974 Taylor visited Canada and in an exhibition match in Toronto scored 349 points in three frames without missing a shot! 1975 was a successful year for the young Irishman, including his reaching the *Pot Black* Final at his first attempt and the semi-finals of the World Championship in Australia. Although defeated by Eddie Charlton, Taylor had, in turn, beaten Perrie Mans, Fred Davis and Gary Owen.

In 1976 he again reached the *Pot Black* Final, winning against Rex Williams, Willie Thorne and Fred Davis. However, John Spencer provided tougher opposition in the Final and Taylor, once more, had to be content with the runner-up prize.

Dennis competed in *Pot Black* in both 1977 and 1978 without reaching the closing stages but fared better in the 1977 World Championship. His victories over Perrie Mans and Doug Mountjoy earned him a place in the semi-finals for the second time in three years. However, although playing with great determination and confidence, he lost to Cliff Thorburn by 18 frames to 16.

As one of the members of the International 'Round Robin' Tournament played in Bombay in the spring of 1979, Dennis was the runner-up to John Spencer. He had been the only player to beat Spencer throughout the competition. The pinnacle of his career to date was reached at Sheffield in the World Championship a few weeks later. Seeded No. 8, Dennis had beaten the young Londoner, Steve Davis, in the first round by a closely fought 13–11. He then produced one of the biggest upsets of form in the Championship by despatching the defending Champion, Ray Reardon, in the quarter-finals 13–8. It is now history that Dennis lost to Welshman Terry Griffiths in the 47-frame Final 24–16, but this event must

rate for Dennis as one of the most 'bitter-sweet' of his snooker achievements so far.

Dennis continued the year with a full engagement diary. He competed in Canada and Bombay again and at home played in most of the main events. He represented Northern Ireland in the State Express World Cup and was a losing semi-finalist to John Virgo in the Coral UK Championship. *Pot Black* 80 included both Dennis and Terry Griffiths in the line-up: in their one meeting, Dennis not only beat the World Champion but, in doing so, scored a break of 87 – the highest in the series! Dennis was beaten twice by countryman Alex Higgins – in the quarter-finals of the Wilson's Classic and in the final of the Tolly Cobbold at the Corn Exchange, Ipswich. He also lost twice to Ray Reardon, in the Benson and Hedges Masters and the British Gold Cup.

Seeded No. 3 for the 1980 World Championship, Dennis had no chance of reaching the Final for the second time when the young Canadian Jim Wych won their second-round match, 13–10. The greatest personal success for Dennis in 1980 was winning the Irish Professional Championship from the title-holder, Alex

117

Higgins, with a 21–15 victory at the Ulster Hall, Belfast. Another satisfying triumph was the Pontin's 'Open' and a prize of £1500 in the inaugural Camber Sands Festival (two days earlier he had lost to Alex Higgins in the Professional contest final).

In June 1980, a small team of British players, including Dennis, travelled to Australia, to compete in the Winfield Masters – a *Pot Black*-style TV competition. Dennis was the runner-up to John Spencer but, in typical Taylor tradition, won the prize for the highest break in the competition.

Since then Dennis has retained his Irish title – against Patsy Fagan – and, with Patsy and Alex Higgins, played for Ireland in the State Express World Cup. Always a player in demand for club exhibitions, Dennis is also a regular competitor in most of the large tournaments. His year included the Champion of Champions, the Pontin's May Festival, the Coral UK, the Benson and Hedges Masters. In the World Championship Dennis was losing 9–11 to Kirk Stevens in the first round when he rallied to take the last four games in a row to win 13–11. However, his second-round match did not go his way as his opponent, Doug Mountjoy, progressed on his way to the Final with a 13–8 victory over the Irishman.

After a promising start in the 1981 Jameson Whiskey Trophy, having defeated Dave Martin, John Virgo and Rex Williams to reach the Final, Dennis discovered his opponent, Steve Davis, to be in devastating form. Dennis lost by 9 frames to nil! He also lost to Doug Mountjoy, 5–4, in the quarter-finals of the Northern Ireland Classic but later had the satisfaction of beating Alex Higgins, 16–13, to win the Irish Professional title for the third year in succession. He was the fifth seed for the 1982 World Championship, but his game against the South African, Silvino Francisco, provided one of the many first-round shock results when he lost by 10 frames to 7. Dennis has now slid down the ranking list to thirteenth place.

Cliff Thorburn

Cliff Thorburn, from Ontario, Canada, was the 1972 North American and Canadian Professional Champion but lost both titles to Bill Werbeniuk in 1973. On his first visit to

England in 1973 he competed in the World Professional Snooker Championship, defeating Dennis Taylor 9–8 in the first round and narrowly losing 15–16 to Rex Williams in the second round. He then entered the Plate Competition and lost 15–16 to John Pulman in the Final. He reached the quarter-finals of the World Open Snooker Championship in November 1973 when he was defeated 2–5.

Thorburn's début on *Pot Black* was hampered by an attack of flu and he did not play at his best until the third game. He won convincingly enough against Jack Rea but did not qualify for the semi-finals.

Thorburn did not progress beyond the first round of the 1974 World Professional Championships. However, he regained his form and confidence later in the year when he won the televised Australian Masters Tournament in Melbourne, beating John Spencer in the Final.

Back in Canada, Thorburn won another major tournament by beating Dennis Taylor of Blackburn by 8 frames to 6 in the Final. Said Taylor, 'Cliff is a very difficult player to beat on his home ground'.

Thorburn is also well suited by the Australian playing conditions as his performance in the 1975 World Championship showed. He defeated *Pot Black* Champion

119

Graham Miles in the second round 15–2 and lost by seven frames to Eddie Charlton in the quarter-finals.

Cliff retained the Canadian Professional title in 1976 from Bill Werbeniuk by 11–1. He lost by 14 frames to 15 against Alex Higgins in the first round of the 1976 World Championship.

Cliff made a big impression with the snooker fans at Sheffield in 1977 when, returning to England for another attempt at the World title, he disposed of Rex Williams, Eddie Charlton and Dennis Taylor to reach the Final against John Spencer. At one point the Canadian held Spencer 18 frames to 18, but then Spencer drew steadily ahead and Cliff conceded the last and final frame with the scores Spencer 25, Thorburn 21.

Cliff's quarter-final game against Eddie Charlton in the 1978 World Championship ended his chances of any further progress when he lost 13 frames to 12 after leading by 12 to 8. Later in the year Cliff won the $6000 first prize in the Open tournament at the Canadian National Exhibition Centre in Toronto by beating the young Londoner, Tony Meo, 17–15. An audience of around 1500 watched the exciting Final in the packed match hall where Cliff Thorburn not only won the title, but was the first Canadian to have his name inscribed on the trophy.

Cliff competed in the Holsten Lager Tournament at Slough in the winter of 1979 but went out in the second round to John Spencer. In one of the frames he sat and watched John take every ball to score a 147 maximum! 'It was an honour to be part of a piece of history' was the Canadian's verdict. On to the World Championship, where Cliff was the No. 5 seed, but lost to John Virgo in the first round 13–10. Some consolation for Cliff came in one winning frame with a break of 125.

In September 1979 Cliff won his third Canadian Open – from the world champion, Terry Griffiths – by the slenderest of margins, 17–16. He returned to England the following month as a member of the Canadian trio for the State Express World Challenge Cup. They were beaten by the England and Australia teams, but Cliff had the distinction of scoring the highest break in the tournament with 126 (against Terry Griffiths). The Canadian and the Welshman met yet again in the 1980 Benson and Hedges Masters where Griffiths, the eventual winner, beat Thorburn 5–3 in the quarter-finals.

As a former finalist in the 1977 World Championship, the odds of 14 to 1 offered against Thorburn before the start of the 1980 Championship were, perhaps, somewhat generous. They rapidly shortened, however, as the 32-year-old Canadian Champion defeated, in turn, Doug Mountjoy, Jim Wych and David Taylor to reach the Final against Alex Higgins. Cliff's first World title, won by 18 frames to 16, was well earned, especially the winner's cheque for £15,000!

With the increased value and attraction of sponsored competitions, Cliff and his Canadian colleagues now find it worthwhile to be almost permanently based in the UK. In September 1980, though, Cliff did return to Canada to defend his Canadian Open title successfully against Terry Griffiths, 17–10, in the Final played in Toronto. Then he and his 'team', Bill Werbeniuk and Kirk Stevens, were the runners-up to Wales in the State Express World Cup at the New London Theatre in October. In the Benson and Hedges Masters in January 1981 Cliff lost in the semi-finals to Alex Higgins, and Terry Griffiths defeated him in the Benson and Hedges Irish Masters, Dublin, again in the semi-finals, in February. Despite three previous appearances in *Pot Black*, Cliff had never reached the Final, but in *Pot Black* 81 he did, winning his first *Pot Black* Trophy against fellow countryman Jim Wych. Back at the Crucible Theatre in Sheffield Cliff was one of the favourites for the World Championship title, but became one of Steve Davis's 'victims', losing to the young Londoner in the semi-finals, 16–10.

Cliff's form declined unexpectedly in the 1981–2 season and he failed to win any major event. He was runner-up to Jimmy White in the Scottish Masters and a semi-finalist in the Yamaha Trophy. His biggest and most upsetting defeat was again delivered by Jimmy White who knocked out the second seed in the first round of the 1982 World Championship by 10 frames to 4. However, Cliff still occupies third place in the current rankings list.

Willie Thorne

When Willie Thorne joined the *Pot Black* team of 1976 at the age of 21, he was the youngest professional yet to appear in the series. He lives in Leicester and started his playing career at the Anstey Conservative Club at the age of thirteen. By seventeen he was an amateur snooker international and, two years later, became the junior Snooker and Billiards Champion.

He has beaten, at one time or another, almost all of Britain's leading amateurs and was the losing finalist in the 1975 National Amateur Championships. He defeated the 1976 *Pot Black* Champion, John Spencer, in the Canadian Open in Toronto in September 1975 – a performance which got his professional career off to a promising start.

Willie found himself somewhat overwhelmed by the opposition in the 1976 *Pot Black* series, but enjoyed a happier time the next year beating Dennis Taylor and Graham Miles and becoming a semi-finalist. He lost to Perrie Mans in the second semi-final and then to Cliff Thorburn in the play-off for third place.

Willie's record in the 1977 and 1978 World Championships was moderate. He was beaten in both his first-round games, by Graham Miles in 1977 and Eddie Charlton in 1978, although it is only fair to say that this last defeat was by the odd frame in twenty-five.

In November 1978 he enjoyed a first-round success against Ray Reardon in the UK Championship, winning 9–6. His next game, in the quarter-finals, was less than satisfying for Willie with a 9–1 defeat by Graham Miles. He narrowly lost 5–4 against Dennis Taylor in the Lucania Pro-Am at Romford, although he scored a break of 116 in the seventh frame, the highest break that had been made by a professional at that particular venue. Willie achieved three similar records during a tour of Scotland including a 140 total clearance on his first visit to the table at the Queen's Club, Glasgow.

In the preliminary round of the 1979 World Championship he had an easy win over Jim Charlton, Eddie's brother, 9–3. His next opponent was John Virgo and this match between two promising professionals turned out to be a minor classic. At one stage Willie was leading 8–5 but Virgo took the next four frames to win 9–8. In the 1979 Coral UK Willie lost his third-round game against Dennis Taylor by 9 frames to 8, after beating Roy Andrewartha, 9–4, in the second. On next to the Padmore/Super Crystalate International where he went one better, defeat-

ing Graham Miles before losing to Alex Higgins in the

semi-finals. His game against Miles included a break of 106. In the British Gold Cup, at Derby, he won two games in the qualifying round, against John Pulman and John Virgo, but once again was denied progress into the semi-finals by Dennis Taylor.

Canadian Bill Werbeniuk put paid to Willie's chances in the 1980 World Championship, 10–9 in the first round after Thorne had won two qualifying matches. But consolation for the Leicester player arrived soon afterwards when, at the Pontin's Festival at Prestatyn, he took the first prize in the 'Open' Tournament, defeating, among others, Steve Davis and, in the final, the former world amateur champion, Cliff Wilson. This 'knock-out' competition played over a week provided him with his first professional title in five years.

Willie is now the proud resident professional at his own Snooker Centre in Charles Street, Leicester. It was at this venue that Susan Foster (Tamworth) won the 1980 Guinness British Women's Championship.

For Willie himself, his performances in the top tournaments were not quite effective enough to involve him in the closing stages. In the Coral UK Championship, November 1980, he beat Jim Meadowcroft 9–1 in the first round, but lost to Alex Higgins in the second. He was a beaten semi-finalist in the John Courage English Professional, 9–8 to Tony Meo, and lost to Doug Mountjoy, 10–6, in the first round of the World Championship. Willie came nearest to playing the winning role when he lost the last frame (by only one point!) against Terry Griffiths in the 9–8 Final in the Pontin's Professional at Prestatyn.

Willie had earned no 'ranking' points during the three years prior to the 1982 World Championship and, not long before that event, had fractured both legs in a 'go-karting' accident! Nevertheless, at Sheffield he provided some of his best snooker ever with first- and second-round victories over Terry Griffiths and John Spencer. This took Willie into the quarter-finals against Alex Higgins, where he scored the highest break of the tournament – a 143 clearance – before losing by 13 frames to 10. Willie was later a welcome guest during the 1982 series of *Junior Pot Black*. He occupies sixteenth position for the 1982–3 season.

John Virgo

Born in Rochdale, Lancs, in March 1946, John Virgo won the British Boys Championship in 1962, the Junior Championship in 1965 and the Youth Championship in 1969. He has been a professional since 1976. Between 1970 and 1976 he played many times for England in the Home Internationals winning the majority of his matches. He defeated the 1978 *Pot Black* Champion Doug Mount-joy in the semi-finals of the 1976 Embassy Amateur International and went on to win his first important tournament. Also in that year he partnered Paul Medati to win two worthwhile amateur pairs competitions – the Joe Coral and the Double Diamond.

Virgo has played in each World Championship since 1977. In that year he lost to John Spencer 13–9 in the first round and in 1978 was narrowly beaten by Fred Davis, 9–8, in the qualifying round. The 1979 Championship proved to be much more satisfactory. John showed his best form to date by winning his game in the preliminary round 9–0 against Maurice Parkin of Sheffield, and the qualifying round tie by 9–8 against Willie Thorne. In the first round, with the pace getting hotter, John beat Cliff Thorburn of Canada 13–10, and another Canadian, Bill Werbeniuk, 13–9 in the quarter-finals. John was now in

the semi-finals of the World Championship for the first time in his career, but lost to Dennis Taylor 19–12. In the play-off for third place between the two losing semi-finalists, Eddie Charlton beat Virgo 7–3.

At the end of 1979, however, John had scored his biggest success since turning professional. At the Guild-hall, Preston, he took the first prize, a trophy and £4500, upon winning the Coral UK Championship. His opponent in the Final was the 1979 World Champion Terry Griffiths and, after a drama-packed contest during which Virgo forfeited two frames to Griffiths for arriving late at a session, the result was Virgo 14 frames, Griffiths 13. 'To say it's the biggest breakthrough in my career is an under-statement' was John's immediate reaction. He maintained his new-found form shortly afterwards, winning the Bombay International Tournament against Cliff Thorburn by 13–7 in a two-day Final.

1980 was not quite so lucky for John as far as the World Championship was concerned. He had an easy win over Jim Meadowcroft in the first round, but his tremendous effort to survive the next ended with a one-frame defeat by Eddie Charlton, 13–12. John's disappointment at losing to Charlton, coupled with 'still feeling in peak condition', resulted in a compensating victory for him within a very short time. At the 1980 Pontin's Professional Tournament at Prestatyn he won the £2000 first prize, beating the two Davises, Fred and Steve, and then Ray Reardon in the Final, 9–6. Virgo made a 96 clearance in the last, winning frame.

At the New London Theatre in October 1980, John beat Kirk Stevens, Dennis Taylor, Steve Davis and Ray Reardon in Group A for the Champion of Champions title. In the Final both he and Doug Mountjoy missed several frame-winning chances, but Mountjoy eventually won 10–8. John competed with less success in the Coral UK, losing to Tony Meo in the second round 9–1, and finished without a win in his group for the Yamaha Organs Trophy. Seeded No. 12, John lost, yet again, to Tony Meo in the first round of the 1981 World Championship by 10 frames to 6.

At Derby, in the spring of 1982, John reached the semi-finals of the Yamaha Trophy, going out to Steve Davis, 2–0. Later, at Sheffield, the thirteenth seed found that figure to be an unlucky omen in the second round when, having previously beaten Mike Hallett, he failed against Ray Reardon by 13 frames to 8. During the televised championship John displayed part of his 'cabaret act' consisting of impersonations of his snooker colleagues. John is ranked nineteenth for the 1983 Championship.

Bill Werbeniuk

'Big Bill', a former Canadian champion, was born in Winnipeg and subsequently lived in Vancouver. He turned professional at the age of 26 in 1973. Throughout the seventies Werbeniuk has been a constant threat to the supremacy of his fellow-countryman, Cliff Thorburn. He is well known as a powerful hitter of the ball, which is understandable when you consider that his weight fluctuates between 16 and 18 stone!

Bill has been a regular visitor to the UK for the past few years and had become a familiar 'figure' to the spectators at the World Snooker Championships in which his performance has been improving over the years. In 1974 and 1976 he did not survive beyond the second rounds, beaten on each occasion by Fred Davis. At Sheffield in April 1978 he defeated John Pulman to gain a place in the

quarter-finals, only to find Ray Reardon too good for him by 13 frames to 6. This experience was, nevertheless, valuable to him and Bill entered the 1979 Championship with increased confidence. After beating Roy Andrew-artha 9–2 in the qualifying round, he caused one of the major sensations of the tournament with his 13–11 victory over former World Champion John Spencer, the No. 4 seed. Bill then met John Virgo in the quarter-finals and, although losing 13–9, the Canadian had the satisfaction of scoring the highest break in the competition (142). This equalled the record of the highest break of 142 in a World Championship by Rex Williams.

Back on his home territory for the 1979 Canadian 'International' Bill was beaten 9–5 by Alex Higgins in the quarter-finals, and he also lost to Perrie Mans in the Padmore/Super Crystalate. He was a semi-finalist in the 1979 Coral UK Championship but was outclassed on this occasion by Terry Griffiths, 9–3. He failed to reach the semi-finals of the British Gold Cup Tournament or to last beyond the second round of the 1980 World Championship, being beaten in each instance by the same player – Ray Reardon.

Bill has resided in England for some time now and was appointed resident professional at promoter Mike Watterson's new club, the Sheffield Snooker Centre, in the summer of 1980.

Playing for Canada, along with Kirk Stevens and Cliff Thorburn, in the State Express World Cup Bill had individual successes in the early stages against Ray Reardon, Doug Mountjoy, Fred Davis, John Virgo and David Taylor. But, in the Final against Wales, he was the loser, in turn, to each of the winning Welsh Team, Reardon, Mountjoy and Griffiths. He lost to Steve Davis, 9–3, in the second round of the Coral UK, and finished last in Group Two of the Yamaha Organs Trophy. Bill fared somewhat better in the 1981 World Championship where as the No. 10 seed he reached the quarter-finals. For the second year running, though, it was Ray Reardon who put the Canadian out of the competition, with a 13 frames to 10 defeat.

'Big Bill' was beaten 5–2 by Dave Martin in the second round of the 1981 Jameson, and by 9–5 against Steve Davis in the quarter-finals of the Coral UK. He was the ninth seed for the 1982 World Championship but, despite his large daily dose of lager, the Canadian exited in the second round, 13–5, against Australian Eddie Charlton. However, he remains in ninth position in the rankings list.

Jimmy White

Jimmy White is possibly the most exciting and promising young snooker star to join the professional firmament since Alex Higgins won the World Championship in 1972. Born in May 1962, he comes from Tooting in South London and at school (where, incidentally, one of his chums was another young professional, Tony Meo) he began to show a preference for learning snooker to more

academic subjects. Eventually his headmaster gave permission for Jimmy to take afternoons off from school and practise at the local billiard hall! By the age of thirteen Jimmy had scored his first century break and at sixteen was a member of the London Team which won the 1978 English Championship. He won the British Boys Snooker Championship in 1977.

In 1979 Jimmy made further major solo efforts winning the English Amateur Southern Championship and then, against the Northern Champion, Dave Martin, the English Amateur Championship outright. This was an event which put him into the record books as the youngest-ever English Amateur Champion, earning the title just a month

129

before his seventeenth birthday. The young left-hander also played for the winning England team in the Home International Championship but his next triumph was again a solo effort. In November 1980 at Launceston, Tasmania, he won the World Amateur title by 11 frames to 2 against Ron Atkins of Australia. He returned home via Calcutta (where he won the Indian Championship) to find that his application to turn professional had been accepted.

Jimmy's professional début was in the Yamaha Organs Trophy at Derby, where he just failed to qualify in his group after beating John Virgo and Cliff Thorburn. As the youngest-ever competitor in the World Championship, he was also far from disgraced in his first-round match, losing by 10 frames to 8 against the eventual Champion, Steve Davis.

In September 1981 Jimmy fully justified the opening statement above with a scintillating performance in the Langs Scottish Masters at the Kelvin Hall, Glasgow. At one stage he was 1–4 down in the Final against Cliff Thorburn (he had already beaten Ray Reardon and Steve Davis!) but then rallied to beat the Canadian by 9 frames to 4 and to take the £8000 first prize. His second major prize was also well fought for in the Northern Ireland Classic, Belfast. Jimmy's 'victims' were Cliff Thorburn, Doug Mountjoy, and Steve Davis in the final.

Jimmy began as the No. 21 seed in the 1982 World Championship and proceeded to beat Cliff Thorburn (yet again) 10–4 in the first round, Perrie Mans 13–6 in the second and Kirk Stevens 13–9 in the quarter-finals. His semi-final game was for many viewers the most entertaining and exciting in the Championship. This epic, albeit swift, struggle against Alex Higgins resulted in the 'Hurricane' taking the last frame, to win 16–15. Jimmy has now risen to tenth position in the 1982 rankings list.

Rex Williams

Midlander Rex Williams reached the 1973 *Pot Black* Final and after a dour struggle was defeated by Australian Eddie Charlton.

Williams was the youngest player ever to win the English Amateur Snooker Championship at the age of 17.

He was already twice Boys Champion at Billiards and Snooker. As a very young professional, Williams quickly established himself as a player to be reckoned with and the outcome was the winning of the World Professional Billiards Championship against Clark McConachy in New Zealand in 1968. He retained his title in 1971 when he defeated Bernard Bennett at Southampton, and again in October 1973 against Jack Karnhem. In September 1974 Rex defended his title successfully once more against Eddie Charlton at Geraldtown in Western Australia and in 1976 at the Aberdeen Chateau in Geelong, Australia, he beat Eddie Charlton for the second time, to remain World Billiards Champion.

Williams is a 'text-book' player and owes much to Joe Davis for instruction and advice. His dedication to technically correct play resulted in the achieving of the maximum break in snooker of 147 no less than four times. One of these breaks made in 1965 is recognised as a world record – an honour he shares with Joe Davis.

Rex has made several serious attempts to win the World Professional Snooker Championship and in the last few years has figured prominently in the closing stages. In 1972 he reached the semi-finals and lost to the eventual champion, Alex Higgins, by 31 frames to 30. A year later Williams was beaten by John Spencer in the quarter-finals, but in 1974 he was in the semi-finals again only to lose against the current *Pot Black* Champion, Graham Miles. Rex was beaten by Alex Higgins yet again in the 1975 quarter-finals and was unable to progress beyond the early rounds against Jim Meadowcroft in 1976, Cliff Thorburn in 1977, and Willie Thorne in 1978.

In the qualifying round of the 1978 Coral UK Snooker Championship Rex trailed 2 frames to 8 against Welshman Terry Griffiths before taking seven frames in succession to win 9–8. An identical score, but this time against him, took him out of the competition against Graham Miles. The UK Professional Billiards Championship staged at the Northern Snooker Centre, Leeds, gave Rex the opportunity to exhibit his superior skills at the 'senior' game. The title had been held by Fred Davis for twenty-eight years, but in February 1979 Fred was a losing semi-finalist. Rex became the new champion after beating John Barrie of Wisbech by 2952 points to 2116 in the Final. However, Rex, whose ambition has always been to win the World Snooker Championship, only succeeded in reaching the qualifying round in 1979, after beating David Greaves of Blackpool, before he was knocked out of the competition by Graham Miles, 9–5.

He was equally unfortunate in the 1980 Championship, suffering a 9–7 defeat in the qualifying round against the young Canadian Jim Wych. In May Rex accepted the challenge from Fred Davis for the World Billiards Championship, a title which he had held since 1968. The match, played in Leeds in the presence of 94-year-old Willie Smith who was World Billiards Champion in 1920, resulted in Rex losing his crown to Fred by 5978 points to 4452. He made another bid to retrieve it in October 1980 at the Brownsover Hall Hotel in Rugby. Played this time on a tournament, instead of a challenge, basis, Rex lost his quarter-final game against Mark Wildman

(Peterborough) by 1476 points to 1415. He regained the United Kingdom Professional Billiards Championship, however, at the Winter Gardens, Margate, in February 1981. The competition, sponsored by Super Crystalate, attracted a dozen entries including Steve Davis, Graham Miles, John Pulman, Jack Karnehm and, of course, Fred Davis. Having beaten Fred in the semi-finals, Rex met Jack Karnehm, the defending champion, in the Final, winning decisively by 1592 points to 1112.

Earlier in the season Rex had also shown a vast improvement in his snooker form by beating both Doug Mountjoy and David Taylor in the Coral UK before a 9–4 defeat by Ray Reardon in the quarter-finals. He disappeared rapidly from the 1981 World Championship, winning against Sid Hood and then losing to Ray Edmonds in a qualifying group. The many facets of billiards and snooker are also displayed by Rex as the manager of a snooker and pool accessories company and a TV commentator. When he finds time to relax, Rex turns to ornithology. In 1982 Rex regained his World Billiards Championship title at the newly opened La Reserve at Sutton Coldfield, beating Mark Wildman of Peterborough, and was re-elected chairman of the World Professional Billiards and Snooker Association Ltd, the professional game's governing body.

MAKE SNOOKER EASY BY LOOKING AHEAD
by Rex Williams

Professional and match-winning snooker to me is not always the compiling of large breaks interspersed with many brilliant pots, but the stringing together of a whole series of shots with the accent throughout on making everything as easy as possible. Probably one of the greatest assets or secrets of any of the champions lies in their uncanny ability to find the weight or strength of any table on which they are required to play. An inch or two out can bring to a quick end what looks like a very promising situation. This, allied to the fact of being able to spot a winning opening, is the difference between a very good player and a great player – although I mustn't forget to mention that you still have to be able to pot!

Almost anyone playing snooker can point to some

fantastic shot which they have brought off at some time or other – a three-cushion 'cocked hat' double, a miraculous escape from a snooker or some dazzling length of the table pot – but the ones I particularly remember are those which have either salvaged a completely wrecked position or paved the way for more.

In this category Diagram 1 illustrates the point of looking ahead. Right at the commencement of the game I was confronted with the position of being able to pot the red along the top cushion. Unfortunately, the black was covered by the only other loose red. I could have elected to stun the red in and gone back down the table via the side cushion, hoping to leave an angle to be able to pot the blue into the centre pocket and crash into the triangle of reds. But even though I was pretty certain of potting the red and achieving a decent enough position on the blue to be able to carry out this manoeuvre I decided against it. Potting the blue into the centre pocket to cannon on the pink/reds is always fraught with danger, and invariably the cue-ball seems to end up near one of the two top corner pockets, with little to follow, and occasionally heartbreakingly in-off into the bargain.

My choice was to pot the red steadily along the cushion, as in Diagram 2, using running side (in this position left-hand side) on the cue-ball to try and glance the red out of the way of the black, leaving an easy pot black into the opposite corner, with a screw into the pack to open it up, and everything, I hope, plain sailing from there on. The danger is in contacting the red too full, but played with care this is a shot that can make the opening to win a frame.

Diagram 3 is another position often facing even the lowliest of club players. It is a perfectly straightforward pot red to leave an easy black into the top corner. Most people tend to pot the red and hope to split the pack from the black, but the secret is to split the pack first with a short sharp punch shot, not too hard, disturbing the couple of outside reds, still leaving the same position on the black, but the balls now well set for the break to continue. A very easy shot – but look what a little foresight has produced!

Inevitably, however, like snooker players the world over, I do have a shot that I will always remember. The place was Cape Town, South Africa, back in 1965, and I

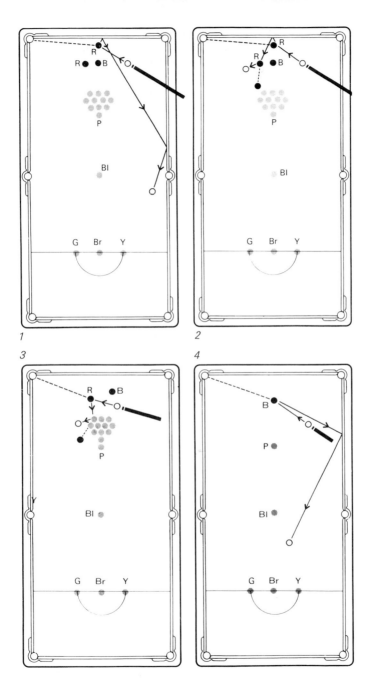

1

2

3

4

was playing the South African champion, Manuel Francisco. This was the occasion when I equalled the world record break of 147. Diagram 4 shows the position I faced having already cleared 14 reds and blacks, just having knocked in the final red. My nerves were definitely unsteady with the record in sight. From a comparatively simple position I had left myself dead straight on the black, needing to get right back dówn the table, which was deadly slow by our standards, on to the yellow. Normally this is not too difficult, but on such a slow-running table, coupled with the fact that my hands were shaking a bit, I thought my chance had gone. However, an almighty screw-shot with acute right-hand side threw the cue-ball off the side cushion exactly as I had planned, leaving absolutely perfect position to mop up the colours. Even the pros suffer with nerves, and on the last few shots the pockets seemed to close up to almost half their usual size. To this day I am still not sure how I managed this shot!

Cliff Wilson

Like Ray Reardon, his rival since the 1950s, Cliff is a native of Tredegar, South Wales. He emerged on the snooker circuit in 1952 at the age of seventeen and twice became the British Junior (Under 19) Champion. He also won the Welsh Amateur Championship in 1956. Cliff soon earned the reputation of being a hard hitter of the ball with a flamboyant, exciting style; his fast, positive, accurate potting won him several amateur championships and he was in constant demand for exhibition matches. His method of play therefore pre-dated that of Alex Higgins by nearly twenty years!

Cliff beat Ray Reardon in the 1954 National Amateur Championship semi-finals, finishing runner-up to Geoff Thompson by 11 frames to 9, but unfortunately he was suffering problems with his eyesight and was forced to abandon the game for many years and turned to other business interests. In the middle 1970s he returned to the snooker table and triumphed in the Welsh Amateur Championship in 1977 and 1979 and also won the World Amateur Championship in Malta in 1978. He turned professional the following year. He lost to fellow Welsh-

man, Doug Mountjoy, in the first round of the 1980 World Championship, 10–6, and by the same score in the corresponding round against David Taylor in 1981. That year he reached the Final of the Woodpecker Welsh Championship where he lost to none other than Ray Reardon. In the 1982 World Championship Cliff won his qualifying match against Paul Medati (Salford) confidently enough, 9–5, but facing the Australian Champion Eddie Charlton in the first round proper, the Welshman took no further part in the contest after a 10–5 defeat. Cliff is well down the 1982 rankings list at No. 27.

Jim Wych

Another young Canadian who hit the headlines during the 1980 World Championship, Jim was born in Calgary   137 in January 1955. He is an all-round sportsman with a degree in physical education, and is more than proficient at golf, tennis, basketball and gymnastics, not to mention snooker! He won the Canadian Amateur Snooker Championship in 1979, having previously also been the 'Central and Western' and Alberta Champion. He then sacrificed the chance to represent Canada in the 1980 World Amateur Championship with the decision to take up the precarious but potentially rewarding life of a professional.

Jim nearly succeeded, at his first attempt, in winning the Canadian Professional Championship in April 1980. He beat Kirk Stevens, 9–7, in the semi-finals but failed to cope with the greater experience of Cliff Thorburn in the final, losing 9–6.

Jim was one of several Canadians to compete in the 1980 World Championship and he beat one of them, John Bear, and Rex Williams in the qualifying section. By winning his first-round game against John Pulman he was now running on parallel lines with his colleague Kirk Stevens. In the second round Jim was in impressive form, beating the 1979 runner-up, Dennis Taylor, 13–10, including a break of 64 in the last frame. By now there were three Canadian players amongst the eight quarter-finalists, but the luck of the draw brought together Jim Wych and the Canadian Champion, Cliff Thorburn. This was the end of Jim's road to the Final, with his senior fellow-countryman winning 13–6.

Nevertheless, it was this performance by Jim which earned him an invitation to compete in *Pot Black* 81 and which resulted in his making a special flight from Canada – missing his Christmas holiday – for the late December recordings. He made the journey worthwhile by winning his games against Eddie Charlton, Alex Higgins and Ray Reardon, to gain a place in the Final. It was no disgrace to finish as runner-up to the 1980 World Champion, fellow Canadian Cliff Thorburn. Wych, who is a left-handed player, suffered a disappointing result in the 1981 World Championship where he failed to produce his previous year's form and lost his first qualifying match to another young professional, Tony Knowles from Bolton. Jim's British engagements have not been as frequent and successful as were to be hoped, and he once again had a disappointing attempt at the 1982 World Championship, losing to fellow Canadian, John Bear, 9–4 in the qualifying round. He is now ranked No. 21 for the 1983 season.

The Syd Lee Story

Born in Streatham, London, in 1910, Sydney Lee was playing billiards and snooker at the age of twelve. After his many successes as an amateur he became a professional in 1939. Syd was *Pot Black*'s referee from 1971 to 1980. During this period his frequent shouts of 'Foul-stroke – Four Away' became almost a catch-phrase among his numerous fans, and he was presented with the *Pot Black* Personality Trophy in 1977 for his contribution to the programme's popularity. Syd says: '*Pot Black* saved the

game of snooker from dying out and has made it the boom sport it is today.'

Unfortunately, ill-health has prevented him from refereeing the series since 1980, but Syd made a welcome return to Pebble Mill in 1982 when he made the presentations in *Junior Pot Black*. With sixty years' experience of the game behind him, Sydney recalls:

'My memories go back to the 1920s when, at 14 years of age, I went in for the Boys Billiards Championship which I was lucky enough to win. I progressed from here into the English Amateur Billiards Championship and won it in 1931 at my second attempt. I was then selected to represent England in Australia and became runner-up in the World Amateur Billiards Championship.

'With the experience gained in Australia, I returned to this country never to be beaten here again and, in 1934, I eventually took the plunge and turned professional. These were the days of great players, like Tom Newman, Tom Reece, Joe Davis, Melbourne Inman and Walter Lindrum. I immediately realised that my class was not with those stars, so put my thoughts to coaching and teaching.

'During the war I became a War Reserve Police

Constable, which allowed me to continue practising snooker. After the war I became the resident professional and coaching instructor at Burroughes and Watts in Soho Square, where I stayed for ten years. I was also touring the country giving exhibitions of snooker against my fellow professionals.

'Some two years after *Pot Black* had been running I was delighted to be invited to become the referee of this very popular programme. The refereeing of *Pot Black* brought me into another field and a new snooker team – Fred Davis, Rex Williams and myself – teamed up to tour the country and, whilst Fred and Rex did the playing, I did the trick shots and the refereeing.

'For those of you interested in trick shots, here are some I invite you to learn and perform to the amazement – I hope – of both yourself and your friends!'

1 — The disappearing trick

Place white ball on pyramid or pink spot with red ball behind white, touching and in line with the lower jaw of the top right-hand pocket. Make sure the balls are touching. Place the cue-ball for an ordinary half ball in off

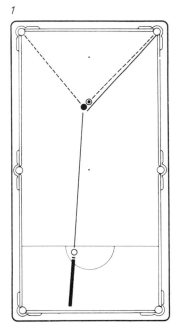

1

from the red into the top right-hand pocket and play the stroke at medium pace. The cue-ball and the white ball will enter the top right-hand pocket and the red ball will be potted into the top left-hand pocket, i.e., three balls into the two top pockets with one stroke.

2—The eight shot at billiards

Place the red ball tight against the angle of the top left-hand pocket as shown and the cue-ball about eight or ten inches from the red and about one inch from the cushion. The object white ball should be placed about two inches from the cushion and just slightly above the centre pocket.

Play a little screw on the cue-ball and strike the red full in the face at medium strength. The red will be double-kissed into the pocket and the cue-ball will rebound to travel down the side cushion, striking the object white and going in off into the centre pocket. This should present little difficulty to the average cue man.

3—The moving cannon

Place a red and a white touching each other about a foot or so up the side cushion and the cue-ball about six inches away as shown in the diagram.

Play to strike the nearest object-ball at about a quarter ball using enough strength and left-hand side to take the cue-ball around the angle as shown. The red ball will travel up the side cushion, meeting the cue-ball just above the centre pocket, thereby making the cannon.

The angles on different cushions can vary and a little practice may be necessary here before you get the correct angle and judgement of strength.

4—The machine-gun shot

This is one to test your speed in cueing. The seven coloured balls are placed as shown in the diagram with a slight arc coming from the green round the 'D'. Cue-ball is placed on the side cushion as illustrated.

The idea is to fire the cue-ball across the table into the bottom pocket, but before the cue-ball drops you must individually pot with your cue the seven other colours as indicated into the same pocket.

5—Pot Black

Firstly, place black on top cushion together with several

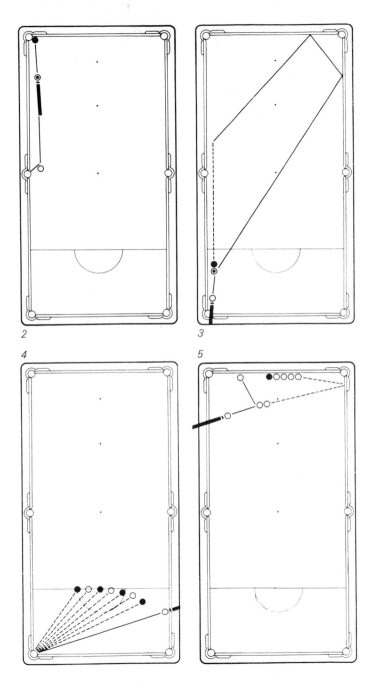

2

3

4

5

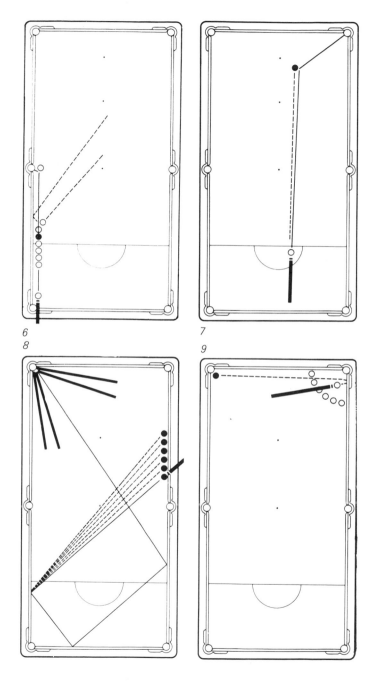

6

7

8

9

other balls as illustrated, all touching one another. You then place a coloured ball between black and top left-hand pocket. The next situation is difficult and will probably have to be tried several times. You make a plant with the two balls just below the black spot so that when struck the plant (as indicated) takes the first ball across the table on to the cushion and back into the coloured balls along the top cushion. Placing cue-ball you then play a cannon from the plant on to the obstructing ball on the top cushion between the black and the top left-hand pocket, so disturbing the ball on the top cushion. By this time the object of the plant will have come up to the back of the pack along the top cushion and will send black into top pocket. This is one to practise but when you have mastered it it is very attractive.

6—Pot Black (another way)

Place a number of colours along the side cushion, and then black, and a further coloured ball the other side going from the baulk end of the table. Place an obstructing ball an inch and a half approximately from the cushion as shown, and then a further ball just over centre pocket.

A cue-ball is placed just above the bottom pocket, again on the side cushion. With considerable force you strike cue-ball into the back of the line of colours. The first colour on the cushion will strike the ball an inch and a half away from the cushion and both balls will go out into the table, leaving a free passage for the black ball to go up to the centre pocket, striking the ball over the centre pocket and dropping into the middle pocket.

7—The moving ball 'in off'

Try this one for fun. Take the red ball and cue-ball in your left hand (if you are right-handed) and at a medium pace push the red ball up the table; at the same time place the cue-ball in the 'D' and when you feel it is time to strike attempt to get in off while the red is still in motion.

You can of course play this shot in reverse by attempting to pot the red once you have mastered the in-off.

8—The steeplechase shot

Firstly take four cues and jam them in the top left-hand pocket so that they are quite firm as illustrated in the diagram. You then take the six coloured balls and place them as shown down the side cushion just above the right-hand centre pocket. The idea is to fire these six colours around the table so that they steeplechase over the cue eventually and into the pocket. The point to watch carefully here is that after striking the first ball you must wait before striking the second until the first ball has struck the third cushion, and so on through the six balls. If you do not get your angles right, although the cues are put there to assist the ball into the pocket, you can easily fall at the first hurdle.

9—The impossible snooker

Imagine your opponent has left you in the situation approximately as shown in the diagram, i.e., all the coloured balls are in a half circle from one cushion round to the other.

Strike the cue-ball sharply as shown onto the cushion where the resilience of the rubber will throw the cue-ball over the offending colours and across the table to pot object-ball sitting over the opposite top pocket.

Ted Lowe

Pot Black 1983 will be my fifteenth year as the 'whispering voice' behind the action. For over thirty years, though, I have been associated with the professional world of snooker. When *Pot Black* began in 1969 it gave continuity to the game I had helped to promote since 1945. It was in that year that I became the General Manager of the Leicester Square Hall in London. Formerly known as Thurston's and destroyed by enemy bombs during the war, it was rebuilt as a new business venture by Bob Jelks, a billiards manufacturer, and two famous players Joe Davis and Sydney Smith. It was in those days that I helped to form the Referees Association – today a thriving body – and was similarly involved with the origination of the Professional Players Association.

It was natural that sporting and show-business personalities should visit Leicester Square Hall to watch the artistic prowess of their fellow professionals. A number were good snooker players themselves, including Sir Gordon Richards, Jim Laker, Denis Compton, Sir Stanley Matthews and the late Sid Field. Television outside

broadcast cameras were often at the Hall and it was also here that my commentating career started. One day, just before the games were due to go 'on the air', the BBC commentator, the late Raymond Glendenning, lost his voice. As I was responsible for helping him to 'read' the play, I was asked to take over the commentary from him. There was no special sound-proof commentary-box then, so I had to sit among the audience and talk quietly into the microphone so as not to disturb the customers or the players. Hence I developed the 'whispering voice' technique.

Over the past eleven years BBC Television have seen snooker become an increasing success in their schedules and today give it a very big coverage as has been demonstrated in the presentation of the World Championships from Sheffield. Such coverage brings interested and enthusiastic sponsors and therefore higher fees for the stars. *Pot Black* can justifiably claim credit for this enhancement of snooker, for it has brought forward the established stars as household names and also created 147 new stars. With the professional game thriving, the trade also enjoys good business and the name of *Pot Black* is now carried by several commercial products.

Snooker was dominated in the late 1960s and early 1970s by Ray Reardon and John Spencer. In the years 1969 to 1971 they won three World Championships and three *Pot Black* Trophies between them. But, in 1972, we invited a 'newcomer' to the series in the talented shape of the Australian Snooker Champion, Eddie Charlton. He won *Pot Black* in 1972 and 1973, with the result that Australian Television became interested in the series and the programme is now regularly rated in their TV Top Ten. Owing to this popularity 'down-under', and as it was evident that my whispered commentary was part of the show, I have been subsequently invited to Australia to compère and commentate on their own snooker series. This series, known as the Masters Tournament and featuring all the top players, is now an annual event together with *Pot Black* on Australian television screens.

Back 'home' in Birmingham, the *Pot Black* office receives a large amount of correspondence from all walks of life – from dear old ladies who admire the good dress and good manners of the players to seven-year-old boys who dream of becoming a future World Champion. It is understandable that the postbag also includes letters of criticism from the inevitable snooker enthusiasts, all of which are appreciated, taken full note of and replied to. May I answer the critics who complain that I talk too much?

Our programmes are usually scheduled for twenty-five minutes and all will know that even with the professional stars some frames can last a lot longer than that. Whilst talking very little over a frame for, say, forty minutes, when the programme is edited to twenty-five minutes, the commentary appears much more concentrated. We will endeavour to give you pleasure without too much interruption!

Throughout my long association with the game I love – snooker has given me many happy times – one man has always stood proud. Alas, we shall no longer have the company of the great Joe Davis at *Pot Black*. He will be missed throughout the snooker world and particularly by me. He was my guide and mentor over thirty-five years. Happy times were also afforded me by the late Horace

Lindrum, to whom I was Best Man some twenty-five years ago, and a number of you will recall that dour Scotsman, Walter Donaldson, twice World Champion and great exponent of the Long Pot.

Today's players are just as great and as much fun to be with or watch. I guarantee the young stars coming along will give just as much pleasure – which is what *Pot Black* aims to do – and I hope that I can 'whisper' to you for a long time to come.

SNOOKER ROULETTE
by Ted Lowe

Whether or not you have a billiards table in your home I am sure most of you will have access to one, and if, like myself and most other players who enjoy the game of snooker, you wish to improve your potting, try this new game called 'Snooker Roulette'.

In a lighter vein, most of us enjoy an evening with our friends around the snooker table, and the introduction of a 'party game' can so often add to the enjoyment of your guests. Again, Snooker Roulette fills the bill. Try it and see whether or not your potting is proficient enough to pot six balls with just six shots. Here are the rules for you:

Game
Shot 1
Spot red ball on 'blue' spot and playing cue-ball from 'D', pot red in top right-hand pocket.
Shot 2
Spot any colour on its own snooker spot and play cue-ball from where it comes to rest in Shot 1. Pot colour into centre right-hand pocket.
Shot 3
Spot red ball on 'blue' spot. Play cue-ball from where it comes to rest in Shot 2. Pot red into bottom right-hand pocket.
Shot 4
Spot any colour on its own snooker spot. Play cue-ball from where it comes to rest in Shot 3. Pot coloured ball into bottom left-hand pocket.
Shot 5
Spot red ball on 'blue' spot. Play cue-ball from where it

comes to rest in Shot 4. Pot red into centre left-hand pocket.

Shot 6

Spot any coloured ball on its own snooker spot. Play cue-ball from where it comes to rest in Shot 5. Pot colour into top left-hand pocket.

Scoring

Twenty points awarded to each pot plus value of ball potted as in snooker.

No pot – no score.

Possible score – 144 points (snooker maximum 147 points).

Alan Weeks
Pot Black Compère

The 1983 series of *Pot Black* will be my fourteenth. No programme I've been involved with has retained – and improved – its popularity with such regularity. Its audience comes from every section of the community; it's perhaps the one sports programme played by men which is now enjoyed equally by lady viewers. 'My wife won't miss *Pot Black*' is a comment I am continually hearing. Proof that over the past decade the programme has made its own contribution to snooker in particular, and sport in general.

My own involvement in sport has taken me through each Winter Olympic Games since 1964, the World Cup since 1962, the Olympic Games since 1960, and the Commonwealth Games since 1970. Yet it was at one of the greatest of sporting festivals that the importance of our BBC Birmingham programme was brought home.

Imagine, if you will, the mighty Olympic swimming stadium in Montreal in the summer of 1976. The building is packed with thousands of people from all corners of the earth. I am making my way to the TV Commentary position where it was to be my privilege to report on David Wilkie winning a Gold Medal in the 200-metres breast-stroke. Suddenly a whole block of spectators rose to their feet, and almost in one voice shouted: 'How's *Pot Black* going, Alan Weeks?' Every person in that block of seats gave me a wave. Where were they from? From Australia,

where the programme enjoys great popularity. In Edmonton, Alberta, during the summer of 1978, I had a similar experience. This time it was New Zealanders attending the Commonwealth Games who were so appreciative.

When I think back to the old BBC Studio at Gosta Green in Birmingham where the programme started its life; when young men like Ray Reardon and John Spencer first made their mark on the way to becoming universally-known personalities; how, with each succeeding year more and more people have wanted to come to see the series made, and its move from Gosta Green to the newer studios in Pebble Mill. What a pleasure it was to have met so many great sportsmen, including the late Joe Davis, whose demeanour and bearing, in victory or defeat, have given the game such a marvellous image.

Yes, when I think back on these things I realise what a privilege it has been to play a small part in one of the real success stories of sport on television.

Professional Snooker Since 1926
by Clive Everton

In 1923, when Snooker was regarded either as a gambling game or a respite from the serious business of billiards, the Billiards Professionals Association, an organisation for markers and professionals attached to clubs rather than the big names of the day, organised a snooker tournament which was won by Tom Dennis, who owned a billiard hall in Nottingham. A year later Dennis wrote to the Billiards Association and Control Council, then the professional as well as amateur governing body, asking them to promote a Professional Snooker Championship. A. Stanley Thorn, the secretary, replied: 'The suggestion will receive consideration at an early date but it seems a little doubtful whether snooker as a spectacular game is sufficiently successful to warrant the successful promotion of such a competition.'

There matters rested until Joe Davis and Bill Camkin, a lively Birmingham billiard trader, had a conversation about the growing popularity of Snooker which led to Davis writing to the BA & CC drafting the conditions under which the event could take place.

The BA & CC gave their gracious consent and took 50% of the entry fees. The players were to make all their own arrangements and take the other 50% though, as it turned out, the BA & CC used that 50% to buy a trophy.

That first championship in 1926 – there were ten entries and Joe Davis netted £6. 10s. 0d. for winning it – did not lead to any dramatic lift-off. Billiards was still the main game and snooker, even the championship, was fitted in here and there. By 1931 the lack of progress was evident from the fact that there were only two entries and Davis defeated Dennis for the title in the back room of Dennis's own pub in Nottingham. The 1934 final, in which Davis beat Tom Newman, was played over three days at Nottingham and two at Kettering.

In 1935, Conrad Stanbury, a burly Canadian, became the first overseas entrant and Davis made the first championship century, 110. Horace Lindrum became the first Australian to enter in 1936 when, with billiards having seriously declined as a public entertainment, snooker took over as the major game, a fact underlined by the *Daily Mail* switching their long-standing sponsorship of a billiards tournament to snooker. Thurston's, the great home of the game in Leicester Square, was able to dust off its long unneeded 'House Full' notices.

The pattern of those seasons in the late 1930s was for Thurston's to stage the championship on a knock-out basis, the *Daily Mail* tournament on an all-play-all system, and week's matches, of which the most popular were Davis *v.* Lindrum. It was considered unthinkable for a really important match to last less than a week and it was hardly considered a match at all if it lasted less than three days. Professionals supplemented their incomes with week's matches in the provinces and one-night club exhibition stands.

This remained the pattern from 1946 until the closure of Leicester Square Hall – the Thurston's match room under another name – in 1955. Though there were other sponsors from time to time, like the *Empire News* and the *Sporting Record*, the great tournament was that sponsored by the *News of the World*. All were contested on a round-robin handicap basis with Joe on scratch, his brother Fred, occasionally on scratch as well, but with other handicaps of as much as 30 points per frame. There weren't enough good players to contemplate doing it any other way.

The 1946 Championship Final, a fortnight's match at the Horticultural Hall, Westminster, had brought snooker to a new peak with Joe, who then retired from Championship play undefeated, and Lindrum sharing an unheard of £3000 for their trouble. Amazingly, in less than ten years professional snooker was to decline from this peak almost to the point of extinction.

Joe's retirement from championship play – when he was still the best player – devalued the Championship and though most of the finals between Fred Davis and Walter Donaldson and Fred and John Pulman brought sizeable spring crowds to Blackpool Tower Circus, one swallow did not make a season. The professionals, perhaps understandably, became preoccupied with simply making a living and there was a sad lack either of long-term planning or new faces.

The advent of television, ironically one of the great factors later in snooker's regrowth, and the closure of Leicester Square Hall, which had provided a year-round shop window for the game, made snooker a tough market in which to make a living. Things went from bad to worse. Disillusioned, Fred retired from championship play and there were only four entries when John Pulman won it in Jersey in 1957. Snooker was occasionally seen on television, usually in the form of Joe v. A. N. Other, but nobody was under any illusion that this was regarded by the BBC or the public as much more than a convenient programme filler. The trouble was, as it was with the professional game as a whole, that all possible permutations of opponents had long since been exhausted and the results were of no significance anyway.

After seven years in limbo, the Championship was revived in 1964 on a challenge basis through the efforts of Rex Williams, who also revived the moribund professional association. Pulman made seven successful world title defences until, for the 1968–9 season, the Championship reverted to a knock-out basis with sponsorship by John Player. For different reasons, three top-quality amateurs had arrived in the professional ranks almost simultaneously in 1967: Gary Owen, twice world amateur champion, John Spencer and Ray Reardon. In Australia, Eddie Charlton had turned professional in 1963 and at least brought a new face to the Championship when he challenged Pulman, albeit unsuccessfully, in 1968. The introduction of colour television, and with it the first *Pot Black* series in 1969, was an invaluable stimulant in these dark days.

Ray Reardon's six World Professional Snooker titles have been won in sharply contrasting circumstances which have illustrated some of the most significant developments in the game of the last few years.

In 1970 he beat John Pulman 39–34 in a week's match at the Victoria Hall, London, after their usual tournament held over several months in different venues, with each match promoted as a separate entity. It was an event typical of almost any year before snooker struck it big.

His next success in 1973 coincided with a radical departure from accepted methods of presenting snooker, when the whole tournament was telescoped into a

Wimbledon-style fortnight with simultaneous play on eight tables. This was an innovation which encouraged much greater audience involvement and created additional psychological factors among the players. It produced an amazing comeback from Reardon, who won eleven of the last fourteen frames to beat John Spencer 23–22 in the semi-final before beating Eddie Charlton 38–32 in the Final.

The 1974 Championship was expected to be an even greater success but it turned out to be a disappointment. The echoing vastness of Belle Vue's Central and Lancaster Halls in Manchester provided an atmosphere far from ideal and there was a promotional disaster when Spencer, the local favourite, failed to survive his opening match against the South African, Perrie Mans. In the same half of the draw, Charlton also lost early and, though this smoothed the way for Graham Miles, the 1974–5 *Pot Black* champion, to reach the Final, he was by that time mentally drained. Reardon beat him easily, 22–12, to retain his title.

The 1975 Championship was staged in Australia and Charlton made a great effort to win the title in front of his own people. He beat the two Canadians, Bill Werbeniuk and Cliff Thorburn, and Dennis Taylor to reach the Final, where he faced Reardon who had come through at the expense of Spencer and Alex Higgins. It was a remarkable contest. Reardon led 16–8, but Charlton won the next nine frames to lead 17–16. Reardon then fought back to lead 22–20, but a winning streak of eight frames in succession put the Australian 28–23 and needing only three of the last ten frames to clinch the title. Again the pendulum swung and, when Charlton missed a not too difficult brown which would have put him 30–25, Reardon's late run began to gather momentum. Eventually it reached 30–30, but Reardon made a break of 62 to win the last frame and the title.

The 1976 Championship Final, for the third time in four years, was held in Manchester, this time at Wythenshawe Forum. Experimentally, the top half of the 16-man draw – after two qualifying events at Southport and Blackpool – was staged in Middlesbrough with the bottom half at Wythenshawe. Ray Reardon began in Middlesbrough with emphatic wins over John Dunning, Dennis Taylor and Perrie Mans, who had become the first South African ever to reach the world semi-final by beating Graham Miles and Jim Meadowcroft. Meanwhile in Manchester Alex Higgins, wayward, unpredictable and exciting as ever, had survived three desperate finishes to reach the Final for the first time since his storybook capture of the title at his first attempt in 1972. He won the last three frames to beat Cliff Thorburn 15–14, and shaved home against John Spencer in another 15–14 finish in the quarters, before beating Charlton 15–13 in the semi-final.

It was Reardon who had to travel for the Final to a venue in which his opponent had been playing for over a week, and it did not make the atmosphere any more harmonious when it was discovered that the match table was far from perfect. Higgins led 4–2 and 10–9 but Reardon always seemed to have enough in reserve for when he really needed it and eventually, as Higgins faded, won very comfortably, 27–16.

In 1977, notwithstanding the fine matches which were contested in the later stages, the match of the tournament came in the first round when Doug Mountjoy, with an amazing final black along the side cushion, beat Alex Higgins 13–12. John Pulman, who had his best championship since he reached the Final in 1970, scored another exciting 13–12 first-round success over Fred Davis, and John Spencer, from 4–7, fought off the challenge of John Virgo, one of several hungry young professionals trying to break into the very top class, 13–9. There was another 13–12 finish in the quarter-finals when Cliff Thorburn, after a 62-minute deciding frame, beat Eddie Charlton; Dennis Taylor reached the semi-final for the second time in three years by beating Mountjoy 13–11; Pulman beat Graham Miles who, since reaching the 1974 Final, had not much distinguished himself in the Championship, 13–10, and sensationally in the result but somewhat tepidly as the match unfolded, Spencer beat Ray Reardon, champion for the previous four years, 13–6.

Down 3–7, Spencer grew stronger as Pulman faded to win their semi-final 18–16 while Thorburn, with a 111 clearance in the penultimate frame, overcame Taylor 18–16 to become the first Canadian ever to reach the Final. For much of the Final, indeed, it looked as if the title could go overseas for the first time as Thorburn led 15–11 before Spencer levelled at 15–15 and went on to win 25–21.

John Spencer in play against Ray Reardon.

Spencer, who had confounded the pundits by winning the title with a two-piece cue which he had first played with only a few weeks previously, did not survive his first match when he came to defend in 1978, for despite breaks of 118 and 138 he was beaten 13–8 by Perrie Mans, a player who had always given him trouble. Higgins, with his instinct for self-destruction leading him to throw away a commanding position, led Patsy Fagan, who had come to the fore by winning the new Super Crystalate United Kingdom Championship earlier in the season, 12–10, only to go down on the final pink 13–12; Charlton, after being within a ball of defeat at 9–12, won the last four frames to beat Willie Thorne 13–12; Reardon, after trailing Mountjoy 2–7, beat him 13–9; and Bill Werbeniuk, a 17-stone Canadian, reached the quarter-finals for the first time by beating an out-of-sorts Pulman, 13–4. In the quarter-finals, Charlton made another miraculous recovery to beat Thorburn 13–12 after trailing 8–12 and Fred Davis, to whom the crowd showed a special affection, reached the semi-final for the first time since 1974 by beating Fagan 13–10; Reardon (13–6 over Werbeniuk) and Mans (13–7 over Miles) won straightforwardly.

The semi-finals brought a moment of anxiety for Reardon as Charlton, after three of their five sessions, led him 12–9, but a 7–0 whitewash transformed the match and prefaced a Reardon victory at 18–14. Davis, despite a

Ray Reardon.

game last-ditch effort, succumbed to Mans 18–16, thus giving South Africa its first-ever finalist.

But the Final saw Reardon triumphantly reassert his position as the greatest player of the modern era. Mans fought hard and at times potted brilliantly but after recovering from 14–18 to 17–18 he could win only one of the last eight frames as Reardon comfortably secured his sixth world title.

With Spencer and Reardon winning the Championship, the vital ingredients of competitiveness and unpredictability were restored to the professional scene. The game, partly through improving amateur standards, became more international. Alex Higgins, winning the World title at his first attempt in 1972, became an exciting new attraction.

The new age of sponsorship brought its benefits, not only in John Player's support of two World Championships but in Park Drive's entry into the sport in 1971 with the promotion of a four-man tournament on a round-robin basis in eighteen different clubs with a televised Final. Park Drive turned its attention to the World Championship in 1973 and 1974, transforming it from a rambling season-long marathon in a wide variety of venues with little continuity of interest into a fortnight-long Wimbledon-style event. Other sponsors, major and minor, cottoned on to snooker's possibilities. Embassy began their association with the World Championship in 1976. Daily television coverage of the Championship was introduced in 1978.

If the seventies had been dominated by Reardon and Spencer, they ended with a new champion and the prospect of a new generation of top players. Terry Griffiths, who only a few months previously had been selling insurance in his native Llanelli, won the World title at his first attempt, a feat described by Fred Davis as 'the greatest achievement the game has ever known'. His quarter-final against Alex Higgins and his semi-final against Eddie Charlton were two of the greatest matches the Championship has seen.

Consecutive centuries helped Higgins to lead 6–2 at the first interval but it was 8–8 going into the final session. It was still level at 12–12 before Griffiths compiled a superb 107 break in the decider. From the quick tempo and sharp shooting of Higgins, Griffiths had to adjust to a war of

Terry Griffiths.

attrition with Charlton. Griffiths led 10–4, was caught at 10–10, and from then on neither man could get clean away. It took a five hours twenty-five minutes final session, finishing at 1.40 am, for Griffiths to secure victory at 19–17 with a climactic final clearance of 97.

Dennis Taylor, who had beaten Reardon 13–8 in the quarter-final and John Virgo 19–12 in the semi, held Griffiths to 15–15 in the Final but could win only one further frame. With a 24–16 victory Griffiths joined the select company of Joe Davis, John Spencer and Alex Higgins as the only players to win the title at their first attempt.

The 1980 Championship confirmed what 1979 had suggested: a new order of top players was emerging. Cliff Thorburn was not, as Griffiths had been, a first-attempt winner, but as a Canadian he broke new ground in becoming the first undisputed champion from overseas. He was held to 10–10 before beating Doug Mountjoy 13–10 to reach the last eight, where a 13–6 victory over his young compatriot Jim Wych, and a 16–7 semi-final defeat of David Taylor, put him into the Final against Higgins – a striking contrast in styles between the measured, calculating Canadian and the explosive, instinctive Irishman. Higgins, resisting his penchant for theatrical coups and spectacular kills in favour of playing

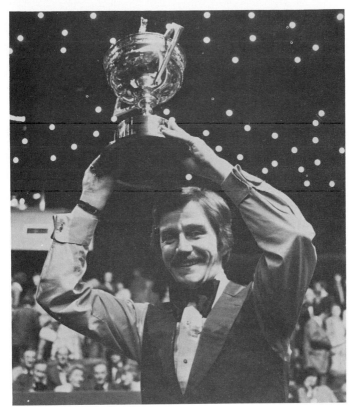

Cliff Thorburn

for keeps, led 9–5 but fatally discarded this sobriety to allow Thorburn the chance to level at 9–9. The second day saw Thorburn fighting not only Higgins but the perverse resistances in himself which, throughout his career, had appeared to afflict him when he was on the brink of an important success. Twice Thorburn missed the pink which would have put him two up instead of level going into the final session; the final black from its spot, the sort he would hardly miss once a month, made the difference between two up and level with five to play; and most heart-lurchingly of all, an easy brown from its spot stayed out when two up with three to play seemed certain. To his eternal credit, Thorburn immediately put this disappointment behind him: a 119-break enabled him to regain the lead, 17–16, and another flawless frame gave him the title.

A third Davis became World champion in 1981. Joe dominated the event before the war, Fred for the decade after it, and Steve, unrelated to the mighty brothers, may well dominate it in the eighties. By no stretch of imagination was he well drawn. His first opponent, the 18-year-old world amateur champion Jimmy White, responded to his chance to make a name for himself in the professional ranks with a spirited recovery which brought him from 4–8 at the start of the final session to within one frame of equality at 8–9. Without a hint of panic, Davis smoothly ran off a break of 71 to clinch the match 10–8. Alex Higgins, who had halted him at the quarter-final stage in 1980, was this time Davis's victim in the last 16. Higgins, looking jaded and publicly confessing his lack of confidence before the Championship, found inspiration hard to come by but nevertheless battled back from 2–6 to 7–9 going into the final session. When Higgins started this with a break of 47, Davis realised the importance of an immediate response. A vital answering break of 45 stopped the Irishman's momentum and helped Davis go to 10–7. A Higgins recovery thus forestalled, Davis closed out the match 13–8 without any great drama developing.

Terry Griffiths, beaten by Davis in 1980 both in the World and UK Championships, held on to 4–4 in their quarter-final but lost several long frames, including two of 57 and 52 minutes, in dropping behind 5–9. The middle session was halted two frames short to allow the match following to start on time but it nevertheless proved a delayed-action killer. Davis went on to win 13–9. Thorburn, who had won ten of the last twelve frames to beat David Taylor 13–6 in the quarter-final, tested Davis's concentration and nerve to the utmost in the semis. Scrooge-like in his safety play, meticulous in considering and addressing each shot, Thorburn led 8–6 after a second session in which Davis lost the last four frames and at one time went over an hour without potting a ball. Remarkably, Davis's confidence remained intact. He patiently won two frames, taking 69 minutes in all, to level at 8–8, and was again level at 9–9 after the Canadian had gone in front through winning a frame which lasted a full hour. It was 12.58 am before the session ended with Davis ahead 12–10. More important, the psychological tide was now running strongly in his favour. He won the first four frames next morning to win 16–10.

Steve Davis

In the opposite half of the draw, Doug Mountjoy, who had never previously reached a World Championship quarter-final, had meanwhile eliminated Willie Thorne 10–6, Eddie Charlton 13–7 and Dennis Taylor 13–8. His 16–10 semi-final victory over Ray Reardon included a break of 145, superseding the World Championship record of 142 jointly held by Rex Williams and Bill Werbeniuk. In the Final, however, he never fully recovered from the disastrous loss of the first six frames. Tenaciously he closed to 5–7 and 7–9, and at 8–10 overnight he was still in contention but Davis, as he had throughout the Championship, started the next session in the high gear more appropriate to a man fully played in and extended his lead to four. Again Mountjoy recovered to two behind at

12–14 to put pressure on the front runner, but Davis nervelessly made breaks of 84 and 119 in the first two frames of the final session and took the next two as well to win 18–12. His prize of £20,000 was the highest in snooker's history and the BBC audience of 15·6 million which watched the live transmission from Sheffield's Crucible Theatre on the first night of the Final was another snooker record.

The Embassy World Professional Snooker Championship 1982

by Clive Everton

It is only a hundred miles from Birmingham to Sheffield, but it seems more like a million from Selly Park British Legion, scene of Alex Higgins's capture of the untelevised, unsponsored World Championship at his first attempt in 1972, and the Crucible Theatre, on whose brilliantly lit stage Higgins became the 1982 Embassy World Professional Champion. For beating John Spencer in the 1972 Final, Higgins received £480. Inflation makes that equivalent fo £1800 in today's money, so the record first prize of £25,000 which he received this time still provides a striking, if rough and ready, contrast in the immediate financial worth of his two World titles.

One can compare, too, the beer-crate-tiered seating at Selly Park with the plush tip-ups of the Crucible, the one public phone in an unlit call-box with the dial-out phones and the television monitors of the Embassy press room, but most of all one can ponder the difference between the 1972 champion – a Snooker star – and the 1982 champion – the kind of Superstar which only television can create.

Prior to the championship Higgins was not, in the inner circles of the game, thought to have a realistic chance of regaining the title. His tournament record for the season had been the poorest of his career and his frustration had surfaced explosively in an altercation with the crowd in his Benson and Hedges Irish Masters semi-final, which resulted in him being fined £1000 by the World Professional Billiards and Snooker Association the day following the championship.

Unforeseeably, Steve Davis and Terry Griffiths, who had hitherto dominated the season, both lost in the first round at Sheffield and Higgins realised that, even below his best, he had at least an even chance with anyone else. Personal ambition alone might have unbalanced him. So often, winning had not been enough for him. He had felt

165

impelled to try and win in the grand manner. This time, he was anchored in reality by his wife Lynn and his 18-month-old daughter Lauren. 'Winning this will set Lynn and Lauren up for life,' he said when it became apparent that he had a real chance. Playing solely for himself his self-destructive tendency might have finished uppermost but, having always lived as if every moment might be his last, Higgins felt, it seemed, perhaps for the first time, that he had a stake in the future to play for. This new sense of responsibility was just strong enough for him to allow the tactician in him to restrain the artist with the love of playing for the gallery.

Alex Higgins with his wife Lynn and daughter Lauren.

For all that, Alex Higgins's compulsive urge to live on life's dangerous edge – stronger than any mere desire to win – had to be satisfied. He led Doug Mountjoy in the second round by two frames with three to play but, as he so often has at the Crucible, squandered winning chances before he proved his nerve in the death or glory situation for which he hungers. After that 13–12 win he again had to recover from two down with three to play in his semi-final against Jimmy White. A break of 72 brought him to only one behind, but it was his 69 clearance, when trailing 0–59 in the following frame, which was so aptly described by BBC summariser John Spencer as 'the break of the tournament'.

The Final was delicately poised at 15–15, level with five to play, but Ray Reardon, who had seemed to be inching towards his seventh title, made two errors, each of which cost him a frame, before Higgins finished the Championship with the flourish of a 135 clearance.

The seventeen-day Championship had produced drama from the very outset as Steve Davis, the defending champion, jaded from an exhausting tournament, exhibition and promotional schedule, was ousted 10–1 by Tony Knowles, who himself suffered the disappointment of a 13–11 quarter-final loss to the durable Australian Eddie Charlton after leading 11–6. The other pre-tournament favourite, Terry Griffiths, also fell at the first fence, 10–6, to Willie Thorne, who went on to make a break of 143, the second highest in the history of the championship, before losing 13–10 to Higgins in the quarter-finals.

Displaying potting and break-building of breathtaking speed and skill, Jimmy White became, at 19, the youngest-ever semi-finalist before going out so dramatically to Higgins. At his first attempt, Silvino Francisco creditably gave South Africa a quarter-finalist by beating Dennis Taylor, the Irish champion, and the 19-year-old *Junior Pot Black* champion Dean Reynolds, who himself made an impressive championship début by beating the veteran former champion Fred Davis.

Embassy World Professional Snooker Championship 1982

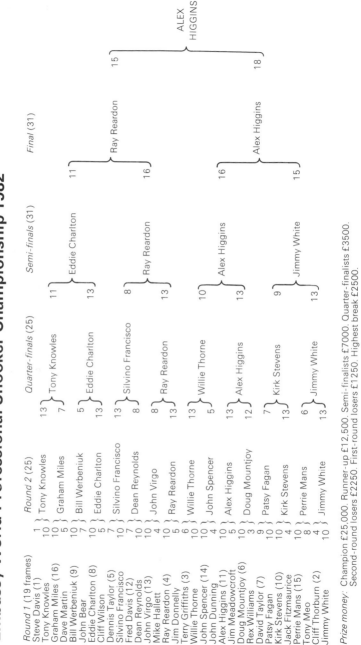

Round 1 (19 frames)		Round 2 (25)	Quarter-finals (25)	Semi-finals (31)	Final (31)	
Steve Davis (1)	1					
Tony Knowles	10	Tony Knowles				
Graham Miles (16)	5	Graham Miles	13			
Dave Martin	10		Tony Knowles			
Bill Werbeniuk (9)	7	Bill Werbeniuk	7			
John Bear	5		5			
Eddie Charlton (8)	10	Eddie Charlton	Eddie Charlton	11		
Cliff Wilson	5		13			
Dennis Taylor (5)	7	Silvino Francisco		Eddie Charlton		
Silvino Francisco	10		13	13		
Fred Davis (12)	7	Dean Reynolds	Silvino Francisco			
Dean Reynolds	10		8		Ray Reardon	15
John Virgo (13)	10	John Virgo		8		
Mike Hallett	4		8	Ray Reardon		
Ray Reardon (4)	10	Ray Reardon	Ray Reardon	13		
Jim Donnelly	5		13			
Terry Griffiths (3)	6	Willie Thorne				ALEX
Willie Thorne	10		Willie Thorne			HIGGINS
John Spencer (14)	10	John Spencer	13			
John Dunning	4		5	10		
Alex Higgins (11)	10	Alex Higgins		Alex Higgins		
Jim Meadowcroft	5		13	13		
Doug Mountjoy (6)	10	Doug Mountjoy	Alex Higgins		Alex Higgins	18
Rex Williams	3		12			
David Taylor (7)	9	Patsy Fagan				
Patsy Fagan	10		7	16		
Kirk Stevens (10)	10	Kirk Stevens	Kirk Stevens			
Jack Fitzmaurice	4		13		Jimmy White	
Perrie Mans (15)	10	Perrie Mans		9		
Tony Meo	8		6	Jimmy White		
Cliff Thorburn (2)	4	Jimmy White	Jimmy White	13		
Jimmy White	10		13			

Prize money: Champion £25,000. Runner-up £12,500. Semi-finalists £7000. Quarter-finalists £3500. Second-round losers £2250. First-round losers £1250. Highest break £2500.

World professional snooker champions

1927–46	Joe Davis		
1947	Walter Donaldson		
1948–49	Fred Davis		
1950	Walter Donaldson		
1951–56*	Fred Davis		
1957	John Pulman		
1958	Fred Davis†		
1964–68	John Pulman		
1969	John Spencer beat	Garry Owen	46–27
1970 (April)	Ray Reardon	John Pulman	39–34
1970 (Nov.)	John Spencer	W. Simpson	42–31
1972	Alex Higgins	John Spencer	37–32
1973	Ray Reardon	Eddie Charlton	38–32
1974	Ray Reardon	Graham Miles	22–12
1975	Ray Reardon	Eddie Charlton	31–30
1976	Ray Reardon	Alex Higgins	27–16
1977	John Spencer	Cliff Thorburn	25–21
1978	Ray Reardon	Perrie Mans	25–18
1979	Terry Griffiths	Dennis Taylor	24–16
1980	Cliff Thorburn	Alex Higgins	18–16
1981	Steve Davis	Doug Mountjoy	18–12
1982	Alex Higgins	Ray Reardon	18–15

* In 1952 the Professional Billiard Players Association dissociated from the Billiards Association and Control Council and organised its own world championship. That year the BA & CC organised its own championship between Horace Lindrum and Clark McConachy, the only two professionals to continue to recognise their jurisdiction over professional events. Lindrum won 94–49. In 1964, the PBPA and the BA & CC reconciled their differences, giving their joint recognition of a world championship on a challenge basis. The system reverted to an open tournament basis in 1969.

† Played in Canada and not officially recognised.

1982 WORLD RANKING LIST

(Calculated on the last three World Championships)

	1980	1981	1982	Total Points
1. Ray Reardon (4)	2	3	4	9
2. Alex Higgins (11)	4	1*	5	8
3. Cliff Thorburn (1)	5	3	0	8
4. Steve Davis (2)	2	5	0	7
5. Eddie Charlton (8)	2	1	3	6
6. Kirk Stevens (10)	3	1	2	6
7. Doug Mountjoy (6)	1	4	1	6
8. David Taylor (7)	3	2	0	5
9. Bill Werbeniuk (9)	1	2	1	4
10. Jimmy White (21)	–	–	3	3
11. Perrie Mans (15)	1	1	1	3
12. John Spencer (14)	1	1	1	3
13. Dennis Taylor (5)	1	2	0	3
14. Terry Griffiths (3)	1	2	0	3
15. Tony Knowles (20)	0	0	2	2
16. Willie Thorne (22)	0	0	2	2
17. Silvino Francisco (–)	–	–	2	2
18. Graham Miles (16)	0	1	1	2
19. John Virgo (13)	1	0	1	2
20. Fred Davis (12)	1	1	0	2
21. Jim Wych (17)	2	0	0	2
22. Dean Reynolds (–)	–	–	1	1
23. Patsy Fagan (27)	0	0	1	1
24. Tony Meo (18)	0	1	0	1
25. John Bear				
26. Cliff Wilson				
27. Dave Martin				
28. Jim Meadowcroft				
29. Jim Donnelly				
30. John Dunning				
31. Mike Hallett				
32. Jack Fitzmaurice				

*Alex Higgins had two ranking points deducted by the W.P.B.S.A. as a 'penalty' in February 1981.

Last year's positions in brackets.

The Elusive 147

The maximum break in snooker is 147 – made by potting a red and the black fifteen times and then the remaining colours in the correct sequence. This total could be extended to 155. If (and it is a big 'if') a player commits a foul stroke before any reds are potted and leaves his opponent snookered, the resultant free ball potted counts as one point, and the black, potted and respotted, gives another seven points before the table is 'cleared' adding another 147 points – 155 in all. To date this total has been purely academic as no player is known to have achieved it. Thus the official world record break still stands at 147.

Although nearly fifty players claim to have made maximum breaks, the strict conditions under which they are subject to scrutiny have resulted in only two maximums being officially ratified by the Billiards and Snooker Control Council. The players were Joe Davis and Rex Williams. Murt O'Donoghue, a New Zealander, was the first to score 147 – on his own club's table at Griffiths, near Sydney, Australia, in September 1934 during a coaching session. In 1941 the late Horace Lindrum, again in Australia, made 147 during an exhibition match, and in 1948 Leo Levitt, a Canadian, scored a maximum in a practice game in Montreal. Yet another New Zealander, Clark McConachy, notched up 147 during a practice game in London in February 1952.

The first officially recognised maximum came, appropriately enough, from the cue of the 'Sultan of Snooker' himself, Joe Davis, in a game against the veteran ex-World Billiards Champion, Willie Smith, at Leicester Square Hall on 22 January 1955. Even then Joe had to wait impatiently for three months before the governing body of the day, the BA & CC, finally agreed that his break could be recognised as a world record.

Ten years later, on 22 December 1965, Rex Williams, a former pupil of Joe Davis, playing against the South African amateur champion Manuel Francisco at a Capetown hotel, also scored 147 and earned the distinction of joining Joe Davis in the record books as holder of the world record break.

John Spencer's successful 147, achieved during the Holsten Lager International at Slough in 1979, was not ratified as a record because the pockets were not deemed to be standard-size. In addition, although the competition was being recorded for television, this particular frame was played whilst the cameras were not in action; and his prize for £500 as the scorer of the highest break in the tournament carried no bonus for being 147. Other sponsors were offering up to £10,000 for the maximum break!

It was left to another Davis – Steve, the 24-year-old South Londoner – to make the first-ever 147 seen on television. The date was 11 January 1982, at the Oldham Civic Centre during the Lada Classic (which, incidentally, Steve lost to Terry Griffiths, 9–8, in the Final). At the

moment of writing Steve has not yet applied to the B & SCC for his break to be officially recognised as another world record. However, apart from the runner-up prize of £3000, Steve's 147 earned him a saloon car. The first person to congratulate him was his opponent, the man whose previous maximum had been 'lost' for ever – John Spencer!

The Women's Game

The fair sex have enjoyed a game of billiards or snooker ever since the games were invented but, not unlike cricket, the sport has been, and still remains, virtually an 'all-male' province. The British Women's Amateur and Professional Billiards and Snooker Championships (where most of the players were on the committee) were held as long ago as 1930 when the first Billiards Champion was Joyce Gardner. In 1948 the then President of the Women's Billiards Association, actress Valerie Hobson, wrote: 'I am looking forward to the time when billiards and snooker will be part of the accepted social and sporting amenities of every recreational centre. . . . Unfortunately there still seems to be some prejudice against women players.'

Despite the campaign successfully waged on behalf of Women's Lib in many other areas, it is only within the last few years that women and snooker have come to be taken seriously. There are still many 'Men Only' clubs where women wishing to play find that they are 'banned' not only from practising on the club tables, but actually from the premises! However, there are now signs that matters are improving and commercial sponsors are beginning to take notice of the attraction of women's competitions and 'Mixed Pairs'. The daily press has also caught on to the growing interest in the distaff side of the game.

The record books are now beginning to contain the names of Lesley McIlrath, 1980 Ladies World Snooker Champion, Sue Foster, British Ladies Snooker Champion, Ann Johnson, Mandy Fisher, Natalie Stelmach, the Canadian Champion, and the 1981 World Champion, Vera Selby from Newcastle, a Grade 'A' referee who was also heard commentating during the BBC transmissions from the 1982 World Championship. More recently Mandy Fisher won a women's open tournament against Sue Foster at Bournemouth which included a 14-year-old – Angela Jones from Poole. A merger is also on the books between the Women's Billiards and Snooker

Vera Selby. *Mandy Fisher.*

Association and the newly-formed World Ladies Billiards and Snooker Association (represented by Vera Selby and Mandy Fisher respectively). There is an ambitious programme for the 1982–3 season which includes several regional championships and the British Open Mixed Pairs.

Junior Pot Black

The mature professional ranks in snooker are rapidly being joined by younger players. Recent examples are Jimmy White, Tony Meo, Kirk Stevens, Jim Wych and, of course, Steve Davis who became the World Champion at the age of 23. It is not too surprising to discover that there are many promising 'juniors' around the ages of seventeen and eighteen who will soon be barking on the heels of their twenty-one-year-old 'seniors'. In 1981 *Junior Pot Black* was devised in an attempt to produce and predict some of the young snooker stars of tomorrow.

From the many applications received from youngsters – whose ages ranged from nine to nineteen – at the *Pot Black* office in Pebble Mill, twelve contestants were chosen. They were all virtually unknown as far as televi-

JUST GETTING
READY FOR
JUNIOR POT BLACK

sion was concerned but had already achieved varying degrees of success in Junior Championships. The twelve players were: Danny Adds, 18, London; Dene O'Kane, 18, Auckland, New Zealand; John Keers, 16, Newcastle-upon-Tyne; Tony Pyle, 18, Exeter; Paul Ennis, 18, Dublin; Mark Bennett, 17, Blackwood, Gwent; Jonathan White, 17, Wolverhampton; Dean Reynolds, 18, Grimsby; Terry Whitthread, 16, London; Neal Foulds, 17, Perivale, Middlesex; Greg Jenkins, 18, Queensland, Australia; and John Parrott, 16, Liverpool.

The series of eight programmes was shown on BBC-2 each Friday from 1 May to 19 June 1981. The 1981 *Junior Pot Black* Champion was Dean Reynolds, and just four weeks after the series was recorded, indeed before the Final was screened, Dean also won the British Junior (Under 19) Championship. Full results were:

Winner: Dean Reynolds (on aggregate scores)
    111–13, 40–66
Runner-up: Dene O'Kane
Highest break in series: John Parrott (98)

The presentations were made by Eddie Charlton and the series was introduced by Alan Weeks, with commentator Ted Lowe, summariser Jack Karnehm and referee John Williams.

Junior Pot Black *1981. Eddie Charlton makes the presentation to Dean Reynolds. Alan Weeks is on the right.*

The 1982 series featured eight players with John Keers, Neal Foulds, Jonathan White and John Parrott reinvited. The other four 'newcomers' were: Paddy Browne, 18, Dublin; Mark Lockwood, 18, Cleckheaton; Steve Ventham, 16, Mitcham; and Chris Hamson, 17, Nottingham. Dean Reynolds, now a professional, returned as a guest. *Pot Black* referee Syd Lee also made a welcome return visit to Pebble Mill to present the winner's trophy. The full results were:

Winner: John Parrott, 77–30, 79–40
Runner-up: John Keers
Highest break in series: John Parrott (56)

Paddy Browne went on to reach the last eight in the World Amateur Championships at Calgary. There were 1048 entries for the 1982 Pontin's Open Tournament. In the semi-finals Ray Reardon beat Neal Foulds but in the final he was defeated by none other than John Parrott, by 7 frames to 3. Both Neal and John were selected to play for England in the home international series, where their team was the runner-up to Wales.

Junior Pot Black *1982. Alan Weeks and Syd Lee with the winner John Parrott (left) and runner-up John Keers.*

Young players interested in joining clubs, entering Junior competitions, or looking for playing facilities in their particular area are invited to write to:

The Development Officer
Billiards and Snooker Control Council
Alexandra Chambers, 32 John William Street
Huddersfield HD1 1BG

The Snooker Year
by Clive Everton

Though the television viewer can enjoy a great deal of first-class Snooker without leaving his favourite armchair, he (or she) cannot thereby form any clear impression of the widely spread and various events which comprise the Snooker and Billiards circuit as a whole. Over the last few years the increase in both the number and variety of events has been dramatic, and the pattern of the circuit is by no means fixed on a year-round basis. There are, however, certain established landmarks. This short summary highlights some of the most important.

1981
September
Jameson Whiskey International

Steve Davis began the new season in the same commanding form that he had finished the previous one by taking the £20,000 first prize in a new £66,500 tournament at Derby Assembly Rooms. ITV networked the last seven days' play. Davis's 9–0 victory over Den..is Taylor in the Final included breaks of 135 and 105 in consecutive frames.

Langs Scottish Masters

Jimmy White, 19, who had become the youngest-ever winner of the World Amateur title a year previously, became the youngest-ever winner of a major professional tournament by beating Ray Reardon, 5–4, Steve Davis, 6–5, and Cliff Thorburn, 9–4, to take the £8000 first prize at the Kelvin Hall, Glasgow. Scotland's most ambitious ever professional tournament was covered by BBC Scotland.

October
Home International Amateur Championship

Wales retained the Home International Amateur Championship at Pontin's, Prestatyn, scene of the six-team tournament for the last four years. Bill Oliver (Plymouth) won the £1500 first prize by beating Ian Williamson (Leeds), 7–5, in the Open Amateur tournament that was held concurrently.

State Express World Team Classic
Wales, champions for the previous two years, were dethroned by England, with Steve Davis playing the starring role in their 4–3 Final victory. A new venue, the Hexagon Theatre, Reading, attracted large and enthusiastic crowds and the event was again covered by BBC Television.

November
Northern Ireland Classic
Jimmy White beat Steve Davis, 11–9, in the Final in the Ulster Hall, Belfast, to earn £5000, his second first prize of the season.

Coral United Kingdom Championship
Steve Davis was at his most commanding in retaining the title with a 9–0 victory over Jimmy White in the semi-final and a 16–3 win over Terry Griffiths in the Final to take the £10,000 first prize. BBC Television covered the last eight days of the championship fortnight from Preston Guildhall.

1982
January
Lada Cars Classic
New sponsors, taking over the slot in the circuit previously filled by the Wilson's Classic, struck gold as Steve Davis immortalised the event by becoming the first player to compile a 147 maximum on television. Granada's scoop was supplemented by a memorable Final in which Davis was beaten 9–8 on the final black by Terry Griffiths to be denied the £5000 first prize.

Benson and Hedges Masters
Steve Davis beat Terry Griffiths, 9–5, in the Final to win £8000 and complete a unique Grand Slam of World, United Kingdom and Masters titles. Tony Meo set a new tournament record break of 136. The event received five days' television coverage by BBC.

February
Tolly Cobbold Classic

Steve Davis took the £2000 first prize by beating Dennis Taylor, 8–3, in the Final. The three-day event at the Corn Exchange, Ipswich, was recorded by Anglia Television.

Woodpecker Welsh Professional Championship

Doug Mountjoy won his national title for the second time in three years by beating Ray Reardon, 9–7, and Terry Griffiths, 9–8, to take the £5000 first prize at Ebbw Vale Leisure Centre. The event was covered by BBC Wales.

March
Yamaha Organs Trophy

A break of 135, a new tournament record, enabled Steve Davis to clinch an 8–7 victory over Terry Griffiths in the Final which provided him with the first prize of £10,000. The event received seven days' network coverage by ITV.

Irish Professional Championship

Dennis Taylor beat Alex Higgins, 16–13, to take the £8500 first prize and retain the title he had held since his successful challenge to Higgins two years previously. The championship abandoned the challenge principle on which it had existed since its inception and all eight Irish professionals competed at the Riverside Theatre, Coleraine.

Scottish Professional Championship

Eddie Sinclair regained the Scottish Professional Championship by beating defending champion Ian Black, 11–7, to take the £1000 first prize in a nine-man tournament at the Glen Pavilion, Dunfermline.

Benson and Hedges Irish Masters

Terry Griffiths beat Steve Davis, 9–5, to complete a hat-trick of titles at Goffs Sales Ring, Kill. The event was televised by Radio Telefis Eireann.

May
Pontin's Festival of Snooker

Snooker's great annual jamboree at Prestatyn saw Steve Davis make some amends for his disappointing performance in the World Championship by beating Ray Reardon, 9–4, to take the £3500 first prize in the professional tournament. Reardon also reached the Final of the Pontin's Open from 1024 entries but found 25 points per frame too great a handicap to concede to the 17-year-old Merseysider John Parrott, who beat him, 7–4, to take the £2000 first prize.

Billiards
World Amateur Championship
This championship is held every two years, alternating with the biennial World Amateur Snooker Championship. Michael Ferreira (India) won the title for the second time by beating Norman Dagley (England) 2725–2631 in an exciting Final at the Sheraton Hotel, New Delhi. In an earlier match Ferreira set three new world amateur records under current rules – a break of 630, a session average of 191.8 per visit, and a two-session average of 123.6 per visit.

World Professional Championship
Rex Williams regained the title by beating Mark Wildman, 3000–1785, to take the £2800 first prize at the La Reserve Club, Sutton Coldfield.